D0196735

EARTH ANGELS

Also by Doreen Virtue

All of the above are available at your local bookstore, or may be ordered by visiting:
Hay House USA: www.hayhouse.com®; Hay House Australia: www.hayhouse.com.au;
Hay House UK: www.hayhouse.co.uk; Hay House South Africa: www.hayhouse.co.za;
Hay House India: www.hayhouseco.in

Doreen's website: www.AngelTherapy.com

EARTH ANGELS

A Pocket Guide for Incarnated Angels, Elementals, Starpeople, Walk-Ins, and Wizards

Doreen Virtue

HAY HOUSE, INC.
Carlsbad, California • New York City
London • Sydney • Johannesburg
Vancouver • Hong Kong • New Delhi

Published and distributed in the United States by: Hay House, Inc.: www.hayhouse.com • *Published and distributed in Australia by:* Hay House Australia Pty. Ltd.: www.hay house.com.au • *Published and distributed in the United Kingdom by:* Hay House UK, Ltd.: www.hayhouse.co.uk • *Published and distributed in the Republic of South Africa by:* Hay House SA (Pty), Ltd.: www.hayhouse.co.za • *Distributed in Canada by:* Raincoast Books: www.raincoast.com • *Published in India by:* Hay House Publishers India: www.hayhouse.co.in

Editorial supervision: Jill Kramer • *Design:* Randal Sargent

Library of Congress Cataloging-in-Publication Data

Virtue, Doreen.
  Earth angels : a pocket guide for incarnated angels, elementals, starpeople, walk-ins, and wizards / by Doreen Virtue.
    p. cm.
  ISBN 1-40190-048-8 (pbk.)
  1. Angels—Miscellanea. I. Title.
  BL477 .V58 2002
  133.9'01'35—dc21

                                        2002004911

ISBN 13: 978-1-4019-0048-9

32 31 30 29 28 27 26 25 24
1st printing, September 2002

Printed in the USA

Contents

A Gentle Note to the Reader

This is not your average book of angel stories, nor a book about angels in the ordinary sense of the word. While people usually think of Earth Angels as do-gooders, this book takes the term literally, as you'll soon see. The material in this book may surprise or even shock those who are accustomed to a more mainstream view of angels.

Some people may mistake the book's intention, thinking that it supports the idea of separation into groups. Yet the information I'm presenting is merely a description of the personality-related, behavioral, and physical characteristics of angels, similar to the type of information found in astrology books. Those who are Earth Angels will relate to the concepts in this book; however, others may misunderstand or even object to the material herein. My intention is to help and to heal, but sometimes such actions create controversy.

←✴→

All of the stories in this book are true, and all of the individuals whose accounts are included here have given written permission for their stories to be published. The names in the book are also real, with the exception of three people who requested a pseudonym, and two who asked that only their initials be published. I'm very grateful to all of them for coming forward and telling their stories, as they have enriched us with their experiences.

Chapter 1

Are You an Earth Angel?

Do you feel different from other people, as if you were dropped off on this planet and wonder when someone's coming to take you home? If so, then you may be an Earth Angel. If you have a passion and talent for healing, teaching, or helping others, yet you yourself have substance-abuse problems, weight issues, relationship challenges, and the like, then you may be an Earth Angel. If you're highly sensitive and you abhor violence in any form, then you may very well be an Earth Angel!

An Earth Angel is a soul with non-Earthly origins. Although all souls originate from the same Divine source, our environment and personal history often shape our personalities and physical characteristics. For instance, those who spend most of their time surfing at tropical beaches will have different looks and mannerisms than people who hole up in their inner-city offices every day.

Similarly, all of the lives you've previously lived have impacted you. And, just as your physical family-of-origin influences you, so does your soul's family-of-origin shape your looks, behavior, and even your life's purpose. Again, the *inside* of everyone is the same: a beautiful, pristine spark of Divine light. However, as a lightworker, *your* spark of light may have spent time in heavenly realms far from our Earth. Those lifetimes that you've logged in the angelic realm, the elemental kingdom, or on other planets have influenced who you are today. Although you inhabit a human body, your soul feels like a traveler in a foreign country—because that is, in essence, what you are.

Not everyone is an Earth Angel, of course—for this role, God called in the biggest and brightest sparks of light for the transition to the New Age of Peace. Those humans who aren't Earth Angels are living lives purely for their own growth, rest, or enjoyment. They may seem dense or decidedly unspiritual, yet they're Divine sparks of life, too. Their lives have simply been dedicated to human, Earthly concerns.

The Earth Angels' Vital Mission

If you're an Earth Angel, then you're a powerful lightworker with a legacy of healing and miracles behind and in front of you. You accepted your Divine assignment to come to Earth and spread your teachings and healing energies. How has your assignment been so far? If you've had difficulty adjusting to Earthly life, then you'll probably find answers, comfort, and guidance by remembering your spiritual origin.

You may discover that you're an Incarnated Angel or Elemental; a Starperson whose past lives have been extraterrestrial (ET); a Walk-In; or a Wise One, which is a reincarnated Sorceress, High-Priestess, or Wizard. You're a seasoned service worker called into action—an Earth Angel. You may have had past lives on Earth as an Incarnated Angel, Elemental, and such, yet you forgot these incarnations, believing that your past lives were human.

The term *Earth Angels* is not to be confused with *Incarnated Angels*, which is one of the five groups of Earth Angels. By learning about your spiritual realm of origin, you'll understand more about your personality, behavior, and individual quirks. As I mentioned, this is similar to the way our astrological sun signs group us into meaningful categories.

My Early Work with Earth Angels

I first accessed information about Earth Angels through my private practice, where I gave angel, mediumship, and psychic readings. My clients usually consisted of lightworkers who were procrastinating with respect to accomplishing their life's mission.

I'll never forget the first Earth Angel I identified during a session. As I scanned her shoulders, looking at her aura and spirit guides, I clairvoyantly saw a large artery-like pole extending upward from her left shoulder. As I looked to see where the pole was attached, I gasped. There, spinning above her, was a hovering etheric spacecraft! I had never had any interests in UFOs or ETs and actually found the whole subject frightening. I hesitated to tell this woman what I saw, but I'd learned to trust my visions and to faithfully deliver them verbatim to my clients. I'd found that, even if *I* didn't understand the visions, my clients usually did.

So I inhaled deeply and blurted out, "I see what may be a spacecraft hovering above you."

"Oh, yes," my client replied matter-of-factly. "It's been with me my whole life." This floored me. However, I listened with an open mind as she explained that the ship was her ever-present guide and protector, watching over her and giving her information when needed. She reported having visited the ship during dreamtime sojourns.

Soon after, I saw several other clients with this same extraterrestrial connection. I've always been one to notice personality and behavioral patterns, so I soon noted that my "Starperson clients" had similar aura colors, facial features, relationship patterns, and life missions.

Discovering the Other Realms

Much of the esoteric information that I receive comes from my own guides and angels, who give me messages while I'm sleeping or during readings or meditations. Through these means, I was told of the other soul-group incarnations to look for in my clients and audience members.

First, I studied the *Incarnated Angels*. These

men and women have angelic faces, heavyset bodies, histories of co-dependent relationships, and are professional helpers. Laurie is a quintessential Incarnated Angel. She's a very sweet and attractive blonde nurse with a large, curvy figure and a heart-shaped face. After years of trying to help her alcoholic husband get sober, Laurie finally made the painful decision to divorce him. Now she's searching for a way to transfer her natural healing abilities to a private practice.

I next noticed the group called the *Incarnated Elementals*. Jayne is a typical member of this clan. With red hair styled in a pixie cut, and a thin, lanky body, Jayne looks like someone who'd wear green elf shoes with curled toes and bell toppings. She's a professional dog groomer and an avid animal-rights advocate who broke off her engagement because her fiancé wanted to move away from the mountains where she grew up.

"He planned to move to the city," Jayne explained. "I'd shrivel up and die if I didn't live near nature—especially if I moved to the city, where trees are practically nonexistent."

The next group that I studied were the *Walk-Ins*. I'd read about Walk-Ins in Ruth Montgomery's books, but the topic wasn't on my mind when I began noticing this group of Earth Angels. A Walk-In is usually a highly enlightened soul who's decided to bypass the usual route of being born and then growing up into an adult body. Instead, the soul negotiates with a human who's unhappy about living on Earth and who's seriously contemplating suicide. Through a lengthy procedure that I'll describe in Chapter 6, the souls exchange places.

Shanti was the first person I met who I was pretty certain was a Walk-In. She didn't remember the soul exchange where her old soul "walked out" and her present soul "walked in"; all she remembers is waking up in the hospital following a car accident. After she recovered physically, her friends and family members frequently remarked, "You're so different now!" Shanti felt as if she were living in the wrong movie. Nothing seemed to fit—not her job, friends, or home. Even her name, which was Robin at the time, seemed all wrong. Over the next year, she changed her first name, quit her job, and moved to New Mexico. Her family still doesn't understand, but Shanti now feels like her life makes sense.

For many years, I assumed that these four categories were the only realms from which Earth Angels originated: Incarnated Angels, Elementals, Starpersons, and Walk-Ins. When I'd discuss these categories with my spiritual counseling students, about 80 percent of them acknowledged an affinity to one of the four groups. I'd even have the students gather into groups with their spiritual clan members. I'd see them crying, laughing together, and exclaiming, "Really? You, too? I'm just like that!" as they swapped stories of Earth life from the perspective of their realm.

But there were always some students who couldn't relate to any of the categories. "What about us humans?" they'd ask.

My son, Grant, finally supplied the answer. He was attending my Angel Therapy Practitioner certification course in North Miami, giving a brief talk to the class about using candles in rituals and incantations. Grant had been studying Wiccan spirituality for some time, and he had a wealth of knowledge to share. At the end of his talk, he turned to the audience and said, "I know what the fifth category of incarnated lightworkers is. . . . I know, because I'm from this category. It's those of us who are Reincarnated Wizards, High-Priestesses, Witches, Sorcerers, and Sorceresses."

A collective gasp rose from the audience, followed by exclamations of, "Yes! That makes so much sense!" and "That's what I am!" Grant's assessment rang true, and it truly struck a chord with the class participants.

Since then, I've studied and interviewed many people from this group, whom I now call the *Wise Ones*. Whenever I lecture or write about the topic, I receive confirmation that this powerful group of lightworkers relates to this category.

Phyllis typifies the members of this group whom I've met and interviewed. She has an oval face and large eyes whose faraway stare speaks of someone who sees beyond the physical universe. She wears her hair long, and she has an elegant, almost regal, demeanor. When Phyllis saw the movies *The Mists of Avalon, The Lord of the Rings,* and *Harry Potter and the Sorcerer's Stone,* she immediately related to the ancient, magical skills that she'd once possessed. Phyllis also knows that she was burned at the stake for being a witch in a prior life.

The Healing Effects of This Knowledge

When I first began publicly discussing this concept, I realized that I was risking being misunderstood, so I limited my discussions to my six-day certification course, because the students who attended were especially open-minded. Even then, I waited until the last day of our course to talk about Incarnated Angels, Elementals, Walk-Ins, Wise Ones, and Starpersons.

Each time that I discussed the information, people expressed tremendous relief, and healing followed. Here is how some Earth Angels surveyed for this book described their reactions to discovering their spiritual origin:

- "Since I found out, I've felt relieved. I no longer feel so strange, and I finally have a sense of belonging."

- "It helps me to know that I'm not the only one feeling this way."

- "I've always known I was different, and now there's an explanation that makes sense."

- "Finally, I realized why I had to help people at all costs. I never knew why I had this drive before."

This healing effect, along with my own guides' urgings and ongoing feeding of information, encouraged me to continue studying this phenomenon.

I had started to write this book several times, yet the moment never seemed quite right—until now—to discuss this topic so openly. I wrote on the subject in one chapter called "Incarnated Angels, Elementals, Starpeople, and Walk-Ins" in my book *Healing with the Angels*. I also wrote an article on the topic, which was reproduced in several metaphysical publications and on my **angeltherapy.com** Website. The chapter and article attracted a great deal of attention, and at every lecture, audience members requested more details, or asked me to identify their Earth Angel realm.

My executive assistant, Bronny Daniels, identified herself as a Starperson the first time I delineated the categories. (Like many Starpeople, Bronny is a Reiki master.) She resonated particularly with the Pleiades (a star cluster in the northern hemisphere), and told me that she twice had spontaneously channeled the Pleideian language.

Immediately following the events of September 11, 2001, I received the angelic message that beings from high galaxies were watching over our planet and had a personal stake in ensuring that

Earth remained intact. If we detonated ourselves in a nuclear explosion, the negative impact would reverberate throughout the Universe. In addition, I got the message that these beings loved us and were watching out for us like guardian angels. Unlike the warmongering images of ETs portrayed in many books and movies, these were loving and compassionate friends.

I requested that Bronny contact incarnated Starpeople around the globe and ask them to join forces with their extraterrestrial cousins. This was the beginning of the Internet-based Starperson's group. Bronny reported that the members felt a strong sense of homecoming. Simultaneously, the requests for more information on the topic of the five realms poured in through letters and audience-member questions. Bronny also strongly suggested that I write this book, and her request finally motivated me to do so, since it felt like the right time.

I wrote a proposal for the book, which I submitted to Hay House, my publisher, and I was told, "We'll talk about it at our upcoming meeting." I started to wonder if this topic might be too weird for them to consider. Bronny and her group prayed that Hay House would agree to publish *Earth*

Angels. And, as you can clearly see as you hold this book in your hands, they did!

Our next step was to survey people who related to the topic of the various Earth Angel incarnations. I first queried my newsletter subscribers, Bronny's Starperson group, and those who had completed my Angel Therapy Practitioner and Certified Spiritual Counselor programs. I figured that I would receive a dozen or so completed surveys. Was I ever surprised to discover that the survey was passed around the Internet, and that I received hundreds of responses!

Characteristics of Earth Angels

There are characteristics that apply to all of the Earth Angels, and also those that are unique to each of the five realms. The chapters that follow describe each realm's individual distinctions, as well as the common denominators that apply to them—including the following:

— **Feeling different, separate, or alienated from others:** Just about every Earth Angel whom I've met, interviewed, or surveyed has said that they feel "different from others." For all of the realms but the Wise Ones, this characteristic continues into adulthood.

Kelly, who is an Incarnated Angel, describes the feeling in this way:

> "I feel like I don't fit in. I always felt that I was a social outcast. When I was in grade school, the other children always told me I was weird. I used to take it extremely personally, and think, *Nobody likes me*. I would sit and cry for hours. I felt so helpless and sorry for myself, because I didn't know why they perceived me as being different.
>
> "I was determined to fit in, and I wanted so badly for everyone to love me. But the only thing that really helped me feel like I belonged was to do things for other people. Later, I became aware of how many people were taking advantage of my niceness.
>
> "Now that I understand my origin as an Incarnated Angel, I'm able to look at situations with a different perspective. It's okay to be different.

It's okay to be me. This is how I'm supposed to be. Now I don't have to do things for people to make them like me."

Many Earth Angels have been teased or verbally abused because of their different appearance, interests, and behavior. As Terry, a Starperson, recalled, "My sisters always introduced me as 'the one who was dropped off by a UFO.'" Now Terry realizes the kernel of truth in her sisters' taunts, and their words no longer sting her.

— **Intense sensitivity to other people, chemicals, or violence in any form.** Earth Angels have difficulty being in crowds, feeling bombarded by the overwhelming emotions and physical sensations emanating from other people. Most Earth Angels have learned to avoid harsh chemicals in their food, cleaning supplies, and toiletries due to distaste and allergic reactions. Violence in any form repels Earth Angels, including arguments, negative media reports, and violent movies. People often tease them for this trait, saying, "You're just too sensitive!" Yet, this sensitivity is a sacred gift that Earth Angels bring to this planet, enabling them to intuitively know where their services are needed. They couldn't turn off their sensitivity if they tried!

Earth Angel Shelly says: "I've always disliked being in crowds, and in places where there's noise and chaos. Quite often, my level of empathy is more of a problem than a blessing. I often feel scattered and disoriented at the slightest raise in energy. I have difficulty living with other people, so I do best when I live alone."

— **A strong sense of purpose.** Even if the Earth Angel doesn't specifically know what his or her purpose is, there's a sense that the mission involves teaching and healing others. As an Earth Angel named Stav put it, "I've always known that my life's mission was to teach, heal, and serve, and to do my part in helping out our troubled world. Although I'm not sure what I signed up for, I'm willing to help."

— **A history of frustrating relationship patterns.** Earth Angels are often raised by emotionally unavailable or abusive parents. As adults, they may attract abusive friends and lovers. Many Earth Angels have love relationships with partners who are unfaithful, physically or verbally abusive, or noncommital. Some Earth Angels are "sent" to dysfunctional families as children to act as healing catalysts. These young Earth Angels feel like adoptees, since they don't relate to their parents or siblings at all. And truly, these are their *physical* families and not their spiritual families. Other Earth Angels sign up for challenging family situations so that they can progress extra fast during one lifetime. Only a strong commitment to understanding and healing this pattern seems to break the spell cast over their subsequent relationships.

— **Strangers telling them their problems, as well as really personal information.** Earth Angels have lifelong histories of being approached by total strangers who ask for help or divulge intimate details of their lives. People often tell Earth Angels, "There's just something about you that I can trust."

Alisann says, "This has happened to me all my life. I can be standing in a room full of people and a person will come over and tell me their most intimate information, without my asking them to." This tendency is especially true among Incarnated Angels, as members of the other realms have learned how they can use their body language to discourage this practice.

— **Looking younger than their chronological years.** Perhaps it's because they eat more healthfully, exercise, and take care of themselves better overall—or maybe it's their spiritual outlook—but Earth Angels often appear younger than their chronological age. Nearly every Earth Angel surveyed reported that people are shocked when they discover their true age. One Earth Angel said that she was carded for buying alcohol until she was well into her 30s.

— **Possibly having a history of personal and familial addictions.** Whether it's food, drugs, alcohol, cigarettes, relationships, or all of the above, some Earth Angels turn to outside substances or influences to numb the pain of feeling different and of being intimidated by their life's mission. One Earth Angel described it in this way: "I found it much easier to cope with life when I used drugs and alcohol. These substances brought me a lightness, or a feeling of numbness, to allow me to forget why I was here. The drugs would put my mission on the back burner. It was more of a worthiness issue back then."

— **A ringing sound in one ear.** Most Earth Angels (though not all) notice a high-pitched ringing sound in one ear. The sound may accompany stressful situations, or come out of the blue. Many Earth Angels consider this an annoying distraction, but the ringing is actually encoded information downloaded from the Earth Angels' realm to help them rise above Earthly problems. It also includes instructions and guidance for the Earth Angels' mission. Fortunately, Earth Angels can mentally ask heaven to reduce the volume or pitch of the sound so that it no longer hurts their ears.

✧❈✧

This is a book for and about *you!* My prayer is that it will help you heal wounds you may have suffered as a result of being different, highly sensitive, extremely creative, or fitting outside the parameters of norms, expectations, and organizations.

Chapter 2

Quiz: What Type of Earth Angel Are You?

Some people know immediately which Earth Angel realm they fit into as soon as they hear the descriptions of each type. But if you're still unsure, this quiz, and the chapters that follow, may help you recognize your spiritual family-of-origin.

Please write True or False (T or F) next to each statement below. Go with the first answer that comes to your mind or heart:

_____ 1. I tend to easily put on extra weight, or I'm currently overweight.

_____ 2. My past or current love partners are addicts or alcoholics.

_____ 3. I rarely break a rule.

_____ 4. I have a hard time saying no.

_____ 5. I highlight, color, or bleach my hair.

_____ 6. I would prefer to help someone one-on-one, rather than in a group setting.

_____ 7. Truth be told, I like animals or plants much better than I like people.

_____ 8. I have Celtic origins, or I look Celtic (that is, I have a reddish tint in my hair, freckles, or a ruddy complexion).

_____ 9. I constantly play practical jokes.

_____ 10. I'm quite the mischief maker, and seem to have a persistent twinkle in my eyes.

_____ 11. I'm fiercely independent and don't like following rules or authority.

_____ 12. My finances seem to be either feast or famine.

_____ 13. I don't like being the center of attention, and I'm usually a wallflower at social functions.

_____ 14. I've always believed in, or been interested in, ETs or UFOs.

15. I'm compulsively thoughtful toward people, whether they express appreciation or not.

_____ 16. I conduct Reiki or other forms of energy or hands-on healing.

_____ 17. My life's mission is more important than getting married and having children.

_____ 18. I really would like to go home now, because I know that Earth *isn't* my home.

_____ 19. I had a life-changing experience, such as a serious accident or near-death experience.

_____ 20. In the past, I was so miserable that I wanted to die and seriously considered (or attempted) suicide.

_____21. I have changed my first name, or I am strongly considering doing so.

_____ 22. My friends and family remark, "You're different now. There's something about you that's not the same."

_____ 23. I have made, or am making, drastic changes to many areas of my life simultaneously (such as moving, changing jobs, and divorcing) all at once.

_____ 24. I have deep spiritual knowledge that didn't come from any books or teachers.

_____ 25. Even though I know I'm different from other people, I still enjoy the company of others and get along pretty well with most people.

_____ 26. I know that I have magical abilities, which are untapped right now.

_____ 27. I have strong past-life memories or interests concerning Arthurian or Atlantean times.

_____ 28. I believe that I was burned at the stake,
       or killed in some other way, during the
       witch hunts or Inquisition.

_____ 29. I have studied Tarot cards or astrology.

_____ 30. I'm very drawn toward Earth-based
       spirituality, such as shamanism or
       full-moon ceremonies.

Scoring:

The number of *true* answers that you noted
may reveal which realm you're from. Count the
number of *true* answers for each successive group-
ing of six questions, beginning with the first six.

- For example, if you answered four or
more *true's* to questions 1 through 6,
then you're probably an Incarnated
Angel. (That is, the more questions you
answered *true* to, the more likely you are
to fit into this category.)

- If you answered four or more *true's*
to questions 7 through 12, then you're
probably an Incarnated Elemental.

- If you responded *true* four or more times to questions 13 through 18, then you're most likely a Starperson.

- If you had four more *true* answers to questions 19 through 24, then you're probably a Walk-In.

- If you answered *true* four or more times to questions 25 through 30, then you're most likely a Wise One.

If your answers don't reflect one particular category over another, then you may be an Evolving Earth Angel or a Dabbler. This is a being who is moving from one realm to another, such as from the Elemental realm into the Starperson realm, a topic discussed in Chapter 8.

Chapter 3

Incarnated Angels

Reports of Incarnated Angels date back at least to the time of Apostle Paul, who wrote to the Hebrews, "Do not forget to entertain strangers, for by so doing, some have unwittingly entertained angels." My books *Angel Visions* and *Angel Visions II* include stories of people who have encountered humans who are Incarnated Angels.

Some angels briefly take on human form to prevent a tragedy, and then vanish without a trace before the humans involved have a chance to say thank you. Yet there are other Incarnated Angels who elect to live their entire lives in a human body—and they're probably among the dearest lightworkers imaginable.

Incarnated Angels tend to:

- have sweet, heart-shaped faces;

- "look" like angels (whether male or female);

- have Cupid-bow lips and large doe-like eyes that radiate innocence and love;

- have overeating or weight issues;

- be a fixed astrological sun sign: Taurus, Leo, Scorpio, or Aquarius;

- be professional helpers, such as teachers, flight attendants, nurses, and counselors;

- lighten or highlight their hair (no matter what their genetic race is);

- have difficulty saying no and feel guilty when others help them;

- love angels; and have collections of angel statues, books, jewelry, etc.;

- have extra guardian angels;

- seem to glow, with a huge aura around them;

- fall in love with someone's potential and try to coach that person to greatness;

- have co-dependent relationships with addicts and alcoholics; and

- stay in relationships much longer than the average person would.

I'm often asked about *Reincarnated Angels.* The term *Incarnated* is more accurate, though, than *Reincarnated.* An angel may have lived more than one life in human form, but if their most recent realms were angelic, the telltale characteristics belie their true spiritual origins.

Many Incarnated Angels struggle with health challenges, especially fibromyalgia, chronic fatigue syndrome, and gynecological problems. Louise L. Hay, the author of *Heal Your Body* (Hay House), says that female health issues stem from "denial of the self and rejecting femininity," and that fibroid tumors and cysts come from "nursing a hurt from a partner, and a blow to the feminine ego."

These symptoms could apply equally well to male and female Incarnated Angels, who look past the surface when they meet people and see their inner talents, Divinity, and potential. Incarnated Angels share these characteristics with angels in the spirit world, who only focus upon inner beauty and urge humans to polish their natural talents in order to make the world a better place.

Incarnated Angels often have friends and lovers who mask their potential with addictions. The Incarnated Angel takes on these relationships as an "assignment," trying to help the person overcome their self-doubts and focus upon their strengths and talents. Unfortunately, this often leads to frustrating relationships for both parties. The Incarnated Angel feels thwarted by trying to heal and fix their partner. And the partner wonders, "Why are you trying to change me?" Many Incarnated Angels fantasize that if they did enough for their partner, or gave their partner enough love, that person would finally heal. This is fine as long as that person believes that a need to heal exists—and is *ready* to heal.

My experience with clients who suffer from gynecological problems and prostate issues is that they also suffer from the "women and men who love too much" syndrome. There's really no such thing as giving too much love. However, when a person gives love and *then resents* the fact that it's not appreciated or reciprocated, the stuffed anger can manifest in physical symptoms.

Many Incarnated Angels have histories of abusive relationships, so if they hold on to toxic emotions related to this abuse, their bodies naturally protest.

Energy, Weight, and Food

A propensity toward chronic fatigue syndrome also provides other clues about the nature of Incarnated Angels. All of the Earth Angel realms are extremely sensitive to energy. Yet, Incarnated Angels may be especially vulnerable to toxic energies and energy drains because of their "women and men who love too much" predilection. The Incarnated Angel is much more people oriented and more likely to work in a large corporation, compared to the other types of Earth Angels.

Incarnated Angels need to practice energy shielding and clearing techniques, as described in the next section. Otherwise, it's like going out into a blizzard without a jacket. An Incarnated Angel named Kelly says that this practice helped her enormously:

> "Whenever a particular co-worker would walk by or stop to talk to me, I would feel absolutely drained. I could swear that he was snatching my energy.
>
> "Soon afterward, I read about some people having 'hooks' in their energy field, where their energy reaches out and takes your own energy from you. After observing that this was occurring, I used the exercises in the book to protect my energy. Shortly thereafter, this man stopped coming around me."

Taking good care of their energy also helps Incarnated Angels avoid using food to boost their vitality. Many Incarnated Angels are compulsive overeaters, and it's very common for Incarnated Angels to carry extra weight on their bodies. Yasmin, an Incarnated Angel, says, "Being a chocoholic provides me with daily, exquisite reminders of heaven, and it's very hard for me to go without chocolate as a result."

Food provides a way for Incarnated Angels to ground themselves when they feel spaced out, and it's also an outlet for stress, especially crunchy, salty foods such as potato chips and popcorn.

It seems that the reason so many Incarnated Angels are overweight is not due to overeating, but because they're energetically shielding themselves with fat. They have difficulty losing weight, even with stringent dieting or exercise. This is especially true among Incarnated Angels who are massage therapists, or who are otherwise engaged in healing touch. They absorb their clients' toxic emotions, and their bodies blow up like sponges absorbing water.

With their voluptuous bodies, exquisitely beautiful faces, and large hairdos, female Incarnated Angels look like plus-size beauty queens. They're often told, "You have such a pretty face. If only you'd lose weight, you'd be gorgeous!" Actresses Delta Burke and Elizabeth Taylor are examples of Incarnated Angels with these physical characteristics.

Male Incarnated Angels are burly teddy-bear types, such as actor John Goodman; or those with sweet and boyish faces, such as actor John Dye (Andrew on the TV program *Touched by an Angel*).

Shielding

Before you step outside into the rain, you put on your jacket. Well, in a similar fashion, it's necessary to put on your "energy jacket" each time you engage in helping another person. When you open your heart toward another, you're also open to receiving residual fear-energy they may spew in your direction. That doesn't mean you shouldn't help. But it's just like helping someone who's been out in the rain for a while: They may have a lot of mud on them, and it doesn't help anybody if that mud transfers to you. In other words, when you help someone clean up their thoughts and emotions, they release the toxins, which may splatter on whoever's near—including you, the helper.

Those of you who are Incarnated Angels tend to be the "bleeding hearts" of the Earth Angel realms, and you particularly need to remember to use shielding techniques prior to conducting any healing work. Otherwise, you're liable to put on extra body fat to protect and insulate yourself. The extra fat doesn't necessarily come from overeating, and you'll find that the weight doesn't budge in response to dieting and exercise. However, the padding is a form of protection that you can swap for a layer of protective energy, or *shielding*.

It only takes a moment to energetically shield yourself. Ideally, you would do this before *any* helping/healing session—whether it's a paid or volunteer session is irrelevant. It also doesn't matter whether the person you're helping is a stranger, a client, a family member, or a friend. And it doesn't matter how long the helping session lasts—it could be a brief moment or several days. Whenever you're about to help someone, shield yourself.

Still, if you forget to shield yourself *before* the session, you can still shield yourself anytime *during* the session. It's never too late to shield yourself; however, by then you may have absorbed some psychic debris, so you'll want to engage in *clearing* afterward. (The next section describes this process.)

Just by holding the intention to shield yourself with a protective layer of light and energy makes it happen. It's done. You really can't do it wrong, or be denied access to the light or energy shield. Anyone who holds this intention receives immediate results, without exception.

Shielding means visualizing, feeling, and/or thinking of yourself surrounded in a cocoon of light. This light is the essence of angels, and it's a living, loving, intelligent entity that you've called to surround and protect you. Don't worry. This light is always of the Divine Light of our Creator. So-called dark forces don't have this light available to share with others (nor would they want to do so even if they could). So, you can't accidentally call in a lower energy when you shield yourself.

You can shield yourself in various colors of light, depending upon your intention. Again, know that your intention to surround yourself with this light won't be denied. Anyone who asks will receive, without exception (although the ego sometimes tries to convince us otherwise, and please don't listen to that voice!). The different colors include the following:

> — **White light:** This invokes the angels around you to surround you without interruption. The angels protect you, and they ensure that you're safe and guarded.

— **Pink light:** This is the light to invoke if you're with a negative person who's obsessed with their problems. The pink light sends loving energy outward toward everyone who talks with you, and simultaneously sends loving energy inward toward yourself. Nothing can permeate this pink shield except loving thoughts and energies.

— **Emerald green light:** See or feel yourself surrounded by this light whenever you want to heal some imbalance in your physical body. Your body absorbs this light wherever it needs healing energy.

— **Purple light:** Imagine yourself shrouded in royal purple light, which elevates your spiritual frequency, enabling you to rise above problems and contact the highest level of Divine guidance. Purple light also bounces away any lower energies, entities, or earthbound spirits.

— **Rainbow light:** See or feel yourself wearing a coat of rainbow stripes,
which boosts your ability to conduct
energy healing work on yourself or
others.

You can shield yourself in layers of multicol-
ored light if you choose, to invoke all of the beneficial effects of the various colors. For instance,
you can visualize a triple layer of light, with white
light first for angelic energy, followed by a layer of
green light for healing, and then purple light to
elevate your consciousness to the highest truth.

You can also use shielding to protect your
loved ones, your home, your vehicles, your city or
country, and the world. Just use the same methods
in order to envision those people, objects, places, or
areas surrounded by healing light.

Clearing

It's possible that you'll forget to shield yourself before a session, so you'll want to regularly
engage in energy clearing in order to wash away the

effects of fear from your own thoughts, or from the thoughts of others. Fatigue is the main symptom of absorbing these lower energies. This type of fatigue doesn't respond to caffeine, naps, or exercise. The sensation of profound tiredness is chronic, because it's coming from sources foreign to your physical body. Don't worry, though: You can easily remove the cause, as well as its effect of fatigue.

After each healing or teaching session, or whenever you feel very tired, use energy clearing techniques. Your own guides and angels may teach you methods that uniquely suit you, but here are some of my favorites:

— **Cutting your cords:** This is an essential step for all healers and teachers. Each of your students and clients attach etheric cords to you when they believe that they need something from you. Then, after your session, they draw energy from you. They may also send toxic energy through the cords *toward* you. This is a mostly unconscious process, although the cords are visible clairvoyantly, and palpable clairsentiently.

To cut the cords, simply say this aloud or mentally:

*"Archangel Michael, please come to
me now and cut the cords of fear that
are draining my energy and vitality."*

If you're truly ready to release these cords,
Archangel Michael will instantly fulfill your
request. Sometimes people hang on to cords
because of an unhealthy "need to be needed."
If this is the case, ask Archangel Michael to
help you release the fears behind such a desire.
(Remember that the archangels can be with
everyone who calls on them simultaneously, and
that they don't have time or space restrictions.)

— **Taking sea-salt baths:** If there's no
ocean nearby to swim in, you can mimic its
healing effects by filling your bathtub with
warm water and sea salts, which are available
at any health-food store or spa. The pure salt
draws out toxic energies from your pores. Be
sure to choose a brand without artificial colors
or synthetic scents so that you don't inadver-
tently introduce more chemicals into your body.

— **Connecting with nature:** Plants and animals provide a welcome respite from artificial lighting, electromagnetic frequencies, ringing telephones, and pressures from other people. Plants also draw negative toxins out of our mental, emotional, and physical bodies. When you feel tired, take a walk outdoors. Also, keep a potted plant next to your bed so that the plant and its fairies can conduct energy clearing work on you while you sleep.

Angels and Assertiveness

Incarnated Angels are born to help and heal, and they come to Earth ready to enact this mission. However, this eagerness can create difficulties if it's unbalanced.

For example, Incarnated Angels carry such optimism about (and love for) humanity that they often have difficulty saying no. Assertiveness training from a counselor, class, or self-help book or tape may be necessary, since many Incarnated Angels say no to themselves in the form of self-denial, while saying yes to everyone else.

Incarnated Angels often apologize for asking

for help, or don't delegate at all, and then resent the fact that no one's helping them and that they have to do all of the work. This can result in a "Martyr/Victim Complex" in which the Incarnated Angels feel like everyone is taking advantage of them instead of realizing they've created the situation. Some Incarnated Angels feel guilty asking for help, even when asking their own guardian angels for assistance, due to a fear of "bothering" them. Sometimes this fear stems from years of being teased or verbally abused. The Incarnated Angels believe that there's something wrong with them, so they don't believe that they deserve help. They may develop a pattern of self-sabotage and push away opportunities.

The way to heal in this area is to reframe the whole topic of "receiving." This means that these Angels need to realize that they can give and help others more if they allow themselves to first receive. For example, if they feel compelled to be healers, they may need a healing center, money for advertising, a computer, or other accoutrements. They may also need extra money to quit a job that takes their time away from their healing practice.

Related to this is that some Earth Angels, including Incarnated Angels, have difficulty accepting money for their healing treatments. This can create a problem in the case of Incarnated Angels who want to quit meaningless jobs on which they're financially dependent. If they'd accept money for spiritual healing or counseling, they could afford to quit their jobs and become full-time healers or teachers.

It's important for client and healer to exchange energy during healing and teaching sessions. In other words, the client or student needs to give something back. This could be money, food, services, or a donation to the healer or teacher's favorite charity. Encouraging a client or student to give back is part of the healing process offered by an Incarnated Angel.

Many Incarnated Angels have "giving and receiving imbalances." The Law of Giving and Receiving means that whenever we give, we automatically receive. It's the flow and the core of the Universe. And clearly, Incarnated Angels spend much of their time giving. In fact, most of them work in helping professions, such as medicine, teaching, counseling, or the travel industry. However, they often block the flow of receiving for themselves through self-sabotage, self-denial, and wasteful spending.

Female energy is receptive energy, and when a female Incarnated Angel gives too much, she can become unbalanced with too much masculine energy. This is also true for male Incarnated Angels. Giving continually, without taking time out for themselves, is another reason why Incarnated Angels may suffer from fatigue.

The affirmations to heal this imbalance are: "I receive good graciously," and "The more that I allow myself to receive, the better able I am to help others." If Incarnated Angels would affirm these words repeatedly, and adopt the habit of self-pampering, they'd be more open to receiving in other ways, such as accepting help with their mission. Healthy Incarnated Angels realize that they accelerate God's plan of peace if they work as a team, asking and receiving help from each other.

Incarnated Angels feel very comfortable following rules, and they may be afraid of breaking them. They are hard workers, often bordering on perfectionism in their careers. In fact, the surveys submitted for this book by Incarnated Angels were painstakingly neat and well organized, in comparison to surveys submitted by the other realms. These characteristics make it comfortable for them to work in institutional or academic settings. Many

Incarnated Angels work for hospitals, school systems, and airlines. Female Incarnated Angels are frequently employed as nurses, teachers, and flight attendants, or any job requiring a loving heart and saintly patience. I've always thought that it was particularly fitting that so many flight attendants are Incarnated Angels, because after all, angels are accustomed to flying!

The Personal Life of Incarnated Angels

Because Incarnated Angels are physically attractive and have big, loving hearts, they rarely have difficulty attracting romantic partners or friends. Their difficulty is in finding *fulfilling* relationships, however. Incarnated Angels often see their romantic partners and their friends as potential clients whom they can help and teach. They approach new relationships with the question, "How can I help this person?"

As mentioned earlier, Incarnated Angels often fall in love with addicts, and then try to fix them. In friendships, they often play the role of counselor. For instance, Incarnated Angels may find themselves listening to their friends' problems for hours.

When they try to talk about their own problems, the friends suddenly end the conversation. This is another instance where the Incarnated Angels' lives are unbalanced as far as giving and receiving. Who listens to *their* troubles?

As mentioned earlier, Incarnated Angels may have been "sent" into dysfunctional families as their guardian angels, so they may feel entirely disconnected from their birth families and even wonder if they were adopted, as they have nothing in common. These people don't feel like "family" to the Incarnated Angels, and in truth, they aren't. The family members are stranger-souls whom the Incarnated Angels volunteered to help by coming into human bodies and living with them.

Most Incarnated Angels are born under a fixed astrological sun sign: Taurus, Leo, Scorpio, and Aquarius. People born under fixed signs are known for their stubbornness, resistance to change, desire to plan ahead, and their need for guarantees about the future. Yet, they're also focused and tenacious workers who take on challenging assignments until they're completed.

With their tendency to see the goodness and potential in others, combined with their fixed sun-sign characteristics, Incarnated Angels often remain in unhealthy relationships. They stay put well past the time when the average person would have left.

Pamela, an Incarnated Angel, describes her love relationship pattern in this way: "I attract men who have a wounded heart and are really in need of healing. I remain optimistic that they'll heal and that my love will transform them, but that doesn't happen. I have a very hard time ending these relationships, and it takes me a long time to process the pain and separation."

Incarnated Angels often commit to relationships quickly, and soon after the first date, they may decide to "go steady," get married or engaged, or live with the new partner. Incarnated Angel Elizabeth says, "I always start to get serious with men right away, although there are things that I don't like about them. I have trouble just dating."

Since Incarnated Angels leap before they look in marriage, and also marry for the first time when they're very young, they may develop a history of multiple marriages or marriage-like relationships. Many Incarnated Angels surveyed for this book were on their third or fourth marriage. They had a new husband or wife every ten years or so. Again, think of Elizabeth Taylor as a quintessential example.

Many Incarnated Angels have difficulty ending

unhealthy relationships with lovers, friends, or abusive family members. Like compulsive gamblers, they think that if they keep trying, eventually the relationship will pay off. Incarnated Angels live by the Golden Rule and don't want to abandon others— since they have a great fear of being abandoned themselves. They're also reluctant to be honest about their needs and feelings. So, Incarnated Angels suffer silently in a relationship, taking out their unhappiness on themselves. Eventually, they reach the point of not being able to take it anymore. That's when the Incarnated Angel either leaves or pushes the other person away.

Incarnated Angels may have unbalanced and unhealthy friendships and love relationships. Friendships are based upon give-and-take, but these types of relationships are usually one-sided, with the Incarnated Angels always being the helpers and never the "helpees." The Incarnated Angels are supposed to be the strong ones in any relationship, and the "friends" are entitled to unlimited free-of-charge counseling, healing sessions, and psychic readings.

Eventually, Incarnated Angels burn out from this type of lopsided "friendship." They realize that their "friends" have no interest in them, except for how the Incarnated Angels can help them. The Incarnated Angels may feel trapped in a mire of guilt, though, as if they're abandoning friends in need. The "law of attraction" also causes them to lose interest in friends who don't share their beliefs.

It helps for Incarnated Angels to have support, especially from other Angels who understand. The 12-step groups Al-Anon and Co-Dependents Anonymous both provide wonderful support for Incarnated Angels trying to heal their relationships. Study groups for *A Course in Miracles* are also powerful places to heal from guilt. Incarnated Angels can probably be found at any event or place involving angels, such as angel seminars, angel shops, or book-study groups that are studying texts about angels.

Every relationship is an "assignment," with the potential for both partners to learn and grow. No one is a victim in relationships—they're all chosen, either consciously or on a soul level.

Incarnated Angel Nicole says:

> "I've been in four marriage-like relationships. All of my relationships have been with men who were emotionally unavailable and abusive,

cheaters, and drug addicts. Although my friends and family thought I was a victim, I knew they could never see what I could in the souls of these men. I knew that on some level, I was helping to raise their vibration.

"My last relationship was the most difficult and painful. One day I was looking out the window and I told God that I could no longer stay in this relationship. In that moment, I heard the angels say to me, 'We know it is painful; please stay a little longer.' I felt completely loved, and had the strength to finish my work with this man. I'm now with a kind man who's my soulmate, and who's on his spiritual path. He knows I'm an Earth Angel, and he loves me just the way I am."

Spread Your Wings and Fly!

An Incarnated Angel's eyes are filled with wide-eyed compassion and love. The reflection of some personal pain is evident, but it's outweighed by the look of Divine Love. Incarnated Angels look past the surface and see the potential within each person. In contrast, an Incarnated Elemental's eyes reflect pure, playful mischief; and a Wise One's eyes have the haunting and faraway look of hard-won lessons.

Incarnated Angels have the classic physical features of angels that artists have captured. They look like angels, whether male or female. With their sweet faces and dispositions, people will call them "Angel" without realizing the profound truth of that statement. As Pamela says, "Many people have come up to me and said, 'You look just like an angel,' or 'You're so angelic.' Often these are people who are not familiar with my work or my love for angels." Many people report clairvoyantly seeing large feathered wings extending from the shoulder blades of Incarnated Angels, and a glowing white light emanating from their bodies.

Like the other Earth Angel realms, it's important for Incarnated Angels to let their lights shine, even if they're afraid of ridicule or rejection. One Incarnated Angel said, "There's a part of me that wants to fold my angel wings and hide my true identity sometimes. This manifests as sometimes not doing my healing work or missing deadlines for advertising my practice."

Yet, when Incarnated Angels spread their wings and fly, it's sheer beauty to behold. Incarnated Angel Judi has realized the importance of surrendering all of her fears to her guardian angels:

> "At this time, I know that I'm definitely on the right path. All of the desires of my heart are being manifested before me now that I've surrendered and released my life to the service of the angels. Nothing can take that away from me ever. My life purpose and my path have never been clearer or more rewarding. I struggled for so many years, and now I feel like I'm floating on a cloud most of the time!"

Life-Path Work for Incarnated Angels

Incarnated Angels are often attracted to the helping professions, and they make wonderful healers and counselors (traditional or nontraditional); schoolteachers; and members of the travel industry. Most Incarnated Angels enjoy one-on-one work more than working with groups or speaking in front of groups. They're very adept at working in large companies, provided that management has a humanitarian work ethic. Incarnated Angels are miserable working for unethical bosses or firms.

Guidance and Suggestions If You're an Incarnated Angel

If you're an Incarnated Angel, you'll have a more peaceful and prosperous time on Earth if you remember to do the following:

— **Shield yourself with energy and light, especially before helping someone.** This will reduce your need to overeat in order to protect yourself with a layer of extra body weight.

— **Wait before saying yes.** Instead of automatically agreeing to every request for help, give yourself time to meditate, and think about whether it's something that truly is part of your mission and your heart's desire. When people ask something of you, tell them, "Let me think about it," or "I'll get back to you on this." These individuals will respect the fact that you're taking care of yourself.

— **Engage in cardiovascular exercise.** This helps in stress and weight management and is important for Incarnated Angels' healthy hearts.

— **Balance your giving and receiving quotas.** Be sure to give *yourself* treats regularly.

— **Drop any rules that restrict your mission.** Notice whether you have personal "rules" you follow without question, such as, "I better not get too successful, or people will be jealous of me and feel pain from this jealousy." Question rules by asking, "Is this rule working *for* my mission or against it?"

— **Delegate.** Ask for help without apologizing.

— **Accept good graciously.** Allow people to give you assistance, presents, and compliments.

— **Play.** Allow your inner child plenty of time to be silly, free, and creative.

⊰✳⊱

Chapter 4

Incarnated Elementals

This is one of the easiest groups to recognize among the five categories. Like the Incarnated Angels, Incarnated Elementals physically look like their namesakes—that is, fairies, elves, pixies, gnomes, leprechauns, mermaids, dolphins, incarnated animals, and unicorns. Besides the guardian angels that we all have, this group has fairies as their protective spirits.

Very often, members of this group have reddish hair (whether it is full-on red, auburn, or strawberry blonde); and a Celtic heritage or appearance, such as a ruddy complexion or freckles.

Angel or Elemental?

Perhaps you saw yourself in the previous chapter about Incarnated Angels. Still, you identify strongly with the descriptions of Elementals. If you're confused about whether you're an Incarnated Angel or an Elemental, here are four questions you can ask yourself to help you distinguish between the two realms:

1. **How do I feel about rules?** If you're an Incarnated Angel, you usually obey rules and get angry at people who break them. However, if you're an Incarnated Elemental, then you can't stand rules and think that people who abide by them are wimps.

2. **Is there mischief in my eyes?** Elementals are fun-loving beings, often practical jokers, and are always looking for a laugh. If you wonder whether you're an Angel or an Elemental, ask a close friend if you have here-comes-trouble eyes. This is a characteristic unique to Elementals.

3. **What type of wings do I have?** Angels have feathered wings, while many Elementals have butterfly or dragonfly wings. The only exceptions are Incarnated Merangels, who are half-angels and half-mermaids; and also incarnated unicorns, who sometimes have feathered, birdlike

wings. These wings are etheric, not physical.

To determine your wing type, either consult a clairvoyant, or go within and feel for yourself. Focus upon your shoulder blades and feel or see (in your mind's eye) whether the wings are large, eaglelike appendages, or more like buzzing and beautiful butterfly or dragonfly wings.

Also, note your body type: Incarnated Elementals have slim bodies (with the exception of voluptous Mer-Angels), fast metabolisms, and sensitive nervous systems; while Incarnated Angels have voluptuous bodies, slow metabolisms, and mellow personalities.

4 **What is my relationship to addictions?** Most Incarnated Angels are co-dependents, while Elementals are the addicts. Elementals love to party; Angels love to rescue! The exception is that many Incarnated Angels are addicted to food.

Other Distinguishing Characteristics

Sometimes Incarnated Elementals are unsure whether they might actually be from the realm of the Wise Ones. That's because Elementals have ancient histories and relationships with wizards, witches, and sorceresses. So the Wise Ones feel very familiar to Incarnated Elementals. After all, the Elementals were there when the witches were burned, so they may have residual pain from that era, even though they themselves weren't killed. They may have memories of the burnings and confuse them with their own recollections. The primary difference is that Elementals are much more playful than Wise Ones, who tend to be extremely serious, or even somber or stern.

In fact, Incarnated Elementals sometimes get themselves into trouble with their wacky sense of humor. Their jokes may be ill timed, offensive, off-color, or just plain inappropriate. But one of the Incarnated Elementals' missions is to get the world to lighten up, smile, and laugh—even at their own expense.

In the spiritual Elemental kingdom, the fairies, elves, and others hold nightly parties filled with dancing, singing, storytelling, and laughter. They know the spiritual value of playfulness and joy! Not surprisingly, their human counterparts also know how to enjoy themselves. Incarnated Elementals often become professional entertainers, including comedians, actors, dancers, and musicians. Some examples are entertainers Carol Burnett, Ellen DeGeneres, Robin Williams, Red Skelton, and Julia Roberts.

Relationship Issues for Incarnated Elementals

The Elementals were tired of humans' assault on nature, animals, and the environment. They couldn't make headway as tiny spiritual beings, so they elected to take on a human life and body to have more power and say-so in cleaning Earth's air, water, and soil; and helping the animals.

Truth be told, Elementals prefer the company of animals or plants to people. They hold an innate anger toward the human race for hurting the planet. Spiritual Elementals are said to be vicious pranksters, but they're only mischievous toward humans who show disrespect for the environment. On the other hand, they love to help humans who recycle, use Earth-friendly cleaning products, treat animals kindly, and respect Mother Nature. Some of the Elementals' practical jokes are passive-aggressive, stemming from their lack of respect for humans' wasteful ways.

In relationships, romantic partners are attracted to Incarnated Elementals because of their comedic, musical, or artistic skills. But after the relationship begins, Incarnated Elementals may be accused of being "bratty," "immature," "noncommital," or "stubborn." They exhibit the same personality traits as tiny elves, fairies, leprechauns, and the like. In the spiritual Elemental kingdom, these beings are often flirtatious and promiscuous. Incarnated Elementals may exhibit these characteristics in their relationships as well.

The Elementals are much less people oriented than Incarnated Angels. They like to associate with people so they can party, but then they want to be left alone afterward. Elementals are also prone to substance abuse and addictions. So, in essence, while Incarnated Angels marry addicts, Incarnated Elementals *are* the addicts.

Many Incarnated Elementals are in helping professions involving people, but usually because they have a "calling" to do so. Like the Hobbit, Frodo, in the book and movie *The Lord of the Rings*, Incarnated Elementals are reluctant heroes who help people because they *have to*, not necessarily because they *want to*.

They need a lot of space and alone time,

especially outside in nature. Elementals can be shy and very private, even though they're extroverted in social gatherings. They appear to be very open about their private lives, yet there's a guardedness that keeps them from revealing their deepest secrets unless they absolutely trust a person—and that's very rare. They may have an "off with their heads" policy about people in their lives. In other words, when Incarnated Elementals are done with a relationship, they're *really* done.

Incarnated Elementals have learned how to signal people when they don't want to be bothered. Evie speaks for many Elementals when she says, "Strangers used to come up to me and tell me their troubles, but I closed off a bit over the years because I had such a problem taking on other people's stuff."

Incarnated Elementals are clowns when they feel comfortable, especially when surrounded by other fun-loving Incarnated Elementals. In dysfunctional families, they may play the role of "mascot," helping the family cheer up and feel better about themselves. Yet, Incarnated Elementals are also sensitive to disapproval, and so may become introverted, shy, or even reclusive at times when they don't feel socially "safe."

Compared to other Earth Angel realms, Incarnated Elementals are a physically robust group, reporting very few health problems, perhaps because Elementals are more apt to spend time outdoors, hiking and exercising in fresh air and sunshine. Or, maybe the Elementals' optimism makes them minimize or deny health concerns. The only noticeable health pattern in the surveys submitted by Incarnated Elementals was a high frequency of depression, and several Incarnated Elementals said they had histories of childhood asthma. This corresponds with reports that fairies and leprechauns are sensitive to airborne chemicals and need to avoid pesticides in their gardens and foods. It could also be claustrophobia from spending too much time indoors, since the Elemental soul needs healthy doses of fresh air.

Manifestation and Magic

The spiritual Elementals know how to manifest all of their needs. This is one reason why they approach their tasks, like tending to flowers, with playful joy. The Elementals know that hard work isn't a necessity in order to create meaningful results—intention and sincerity are more important.

Incarnated Elementals often eschew hard work, and may be perceived as slackers who favor socializing instead of working. They unconsciously recall lifetimes in the spiritual Elemental kingdom where they could manifest material needs (food, clothing, gold, housing, and so on) out of thin air.

As a result, many Incarnated Elementals feel off-center in the workaday world of human beings, and they begin to manifest poverty for themselves. The Incarnated Elementals whom I've met seem to either create feast or famine. I rarely meet Incarnated Elementals who have achieved financial security unless they're consciously working a process of manifestation, such as the one outlined in John Randolph Price's *The Abundance Book* (Hay House). Then the magic begins! Elementals— like the Wise Ones realm—have magical manifestation abilities. When harnessed, these abilities can bend time and physical laws, and create rapid manifestations and miracles.

Incarnated Elementals have fairies, elves, or leprechauns with them as spirit guides, and they can call upon these benevolent helpers at any time by thinking the thought, *Please help me!*

Elementals and Nature

Most Incarnated Elementals are born under an "earth" or a "water" astrological sun sign, which includes Taurus, Capricorn, Virgo, Cancer, Pisces, and Scorpio. They are truly people of the earth and her spirit. They have great difficulty being indoors for long.

While Incarnated Angels are comfortable working in large windowless buildings, it would be death to an Incarnated Elemental. They *must* be outside in nature or they become depressed. The happiest Elementals are those who create outdoor jobs, such as leading nature hikes or retreats, working at plant nurseries, working as forest rangers, gardening, or dog-walking, for example.

If Incarnated Elementals must work indoors, they should be sure to request the office with a window facing a park or grassy area. Similarly, Elementals are happiest with offices that are crammed with potted trees, plants, and flowers. Playing recordings of nature sounds, such as singing birds, the ocean surf, rain, and the like is also beneficial. In addition, their offices should sport photos of their favorite pets, and statues of fairies and elves. Aromatherapy with genuine (not synthetic) essential oils of plants and flowers helps Elementals stay connected to Mother Earth when they're indoors. (These oils are available at most health-food stores or metaphysical book-stores.)

During break times, it's a wonderful idea for Incarnated Elementals to walk outdoors, even in inclement weather. Elementals need fresh air more than any of the other realms, and those who work in industrial areas devoid of trees and grass can spend time looking at the cloud formations, since Elementals need visual contact with the beauty of the great outdoors. Nature and the outdoors is their church—it's where Incarnated Elementals feel closest to God. An Incarnated Elemental named C.C. says:

> "I get so energized and refreshed in any woodsy, watery spot. I sit under a tree and can feel the good earth energy come right up through my root chakra. I feel safest when I can truly be myself without any inter-ruptions except the gentle touch of a breeze or the sound of birds singing their melodies. The scent of the forest

seems to empower me and gives me a
natural high. I feel like I can conquer
all when I'm there. It's a communion
with nature at its best. The warmth of
the sun is so healing. It's so special
and such a privilege to have nature
share her wealth of knowledge with
me. I'm able to forget all those mun-
dane, everyday things. I can regroup
and re-center. You just can't get that
in a populated area, not even in my
sacred garden place at home. It's not
the same."

Most Incarnated Elementals surveyed could
point out specific natural environments where they
wanted to live, while the other realms were more
flexible about what type of area they resided in.
Almost all of the Incarnated Elementals remarked,
"I *have* to live in the desert," "I *must* be near the
ocean," "I *need* to live in the country," and so forth.

As mentioned earlier, Incarnated Elementals
prefer the company of animals, plants, flowers, or
nature to that of other people. One Incarnated
Elemental recalled her childhood:

"I never was the popular one,
that's for sure. I loved nature and animals and still do. I spent hours playing
under the 17 spruce trees that lined
our property. I even counted them
every day to be sure they were always
there. I preferred nature in my play. I
loved babbling brooks and jumping
from stone to stone."

Deep down, Elementals are angry at people for
being so unkind to the earth and so passive about its
cleanup. The exception is if they find an understanding and playful companion, often in the form
of another Incarnated Elemental.

Since Elementals decide to incarnate to wield
more power in helping the plant, mineral, and animal kingdoms, their life purposes almost always
involve environmentalism or animal rights. This
might mean teaching these values to others, or
through direct involvement in campaigns, research,
care, or cleanup.

In fact, it's important for Incarnated Elementals to get involved in some environmental or animal-rights cause or occupation to feel meaning in

life. In addition, Elementals feel best about themselves if they take personal steps toward bettering
the environment, such as recycling, or using gentle
cleaning products found in health-food stores.

When I asked one Incarnated Elemental what
she considered her life purpose, her reply reflected
many of the Elementals I've met and interviewed:

> "My mission is to teach people
> about protecting the earth and the
> creatures who live here. I see difficul-
> ty for the planet because of man's
> greed and self-importance. We must
> do all we can to save the plants and
> animals before it's too late. So much
> has been lost. So much is in danger.
> Many of our fellow creatures are run-
> ning out of time because of man
> thinking that he's better than the other
> creatures. If we continue to bulldoze
> and build, throw away and extermi-
> nate, we won't be thanked for the
> wasteland that's left."

Every Earth Angel realm displays high levels of creativity. It's logical, then, that Incarnated Elementals make artistic objects from nature. One Incarnated Fairy told me, "I enjoy using flower pods, leaves, pine cones, nuts, and dried flowers to make decorations and ornaments. I've made miniature habitations and furniture outdoors for the little people since I was a child."

Fiercely Protective of Nature

Since the Elementals are God's nature angels, it's no surprise that Incarnated Elementals become almost maniacally protective of animals, plants, soil, and water. Many of the Incarnated Elementals surveyed for this book told me that they had risked personal injury or retaliation in order to protect an animal, tree, or other element of nature:

E.J. writes, "I get angry when others disrespect Mother Earth and her creatures. If, while driving my car, one of my friends throws a cigarette out the window, I pull the car over and make them pick up their cigarette and dispose of it the right way."

Devon (not her real name) recalls:

"I was sitting in my beautiful office one sunny day, which has floor-to-ceiling picture windows. I was staring out at the lovely trees, bushes, and rolling hills just beyond the parking lot, and I noticed a strange pickup truck pulling up. A man who didn't work in our building had stopped in our lot to eat his lunch. That was not a problem.

"However, when he threw his tall plastic beverage container into a flowering bush near his truck, it was as if a human being had been slapped. When I saw this, some type of primal rage boiled in me (I'm normally a quiet, calm, laid-back person). I grabbed a co-worker, and hissed, 'Come outside with me!' I guess I wanted moral support for what I was about to do.

"I ran out to the guy's truck, yelling, 'What kind of person are you to throw trash into a bush?!' He just sneered at me. I ran down the brush-covered slope (with bare legs) and retrieved the cup, scratching my legs all the while. In a moment of unbridled anger, I threw the cup into the open window of his truck, and yelled at him to leave immediately or I'd call the police. He screeched out of the parking lot, screaming foul epithets at me as he drove away.

"My co-worker just looked at me in shock, as she'd never seen me act this way in the five years she'd known me. She said, 'That's crazy! He could have pulled out a gun and shot you!'

"I realized that she was right, but I didn't care. I would not allow my friend, the flowering bush, to be treated in that way—not while I was a witness to it."

Pamela recalls:

"Around the age of 19, I became aware of being one with nature. I had sprayed a bee caught in the windowsill with window cleaner and was suddenly struck by the thought, *What right do I have to kill it?* I immediately took the bee outside to the front of the house, laid it on the ground, and began to rinse it off with water. My mother thought I was crazy, leaning reverently over a dead bee, trying to resuscitate it. From that point on, I didn't kill bugs anymore. Recently, I gently swept up a swarm of ants in my apartment with a broom and put them outside. Then I politely requested that the ants no longer return, and a week later they stopped coming."

The Different Types of Elementals

As mentioned earlier, Incarnated Elementals look just like their counterparts in the spiritual Elemental world. They are larger versions of fairies, pixies, leprechauns, and so on. Here are some examples of the various types of Elementals:

— **Fairies:** Jenny is five feet tall, with a slim figure, pretty face, large eyes, and long wavy hair that falls to her lower back. Everything about her screams, "Fairy!" and Jenny looks like she could be a model for fairy paintings and statues. She is also sweet, unassuming, and shy—just like a fairy. In fact, Jenny is so connected with the fairy realm that she gives professional angel and fairy readings, often using my *Healing with the Fairies Oracle Cards*. She advises her clients to spend time in nature to recharge their energy, and adds, "Remember to call on the angels and fairies continually to help you with every aspect of your life and mission. Also, take yourself lightly—don't get too serious! Ask the fairies to help you add enchantment and magic to your everyday experiences and your life in general.'"

— **Pixies, elves, and brownies:** Evie is a professional singer/songwriter with a ski-slope nose and short dark hair. She says, "People say I look like a pixie. My nicknames when I was young were, 'Tinkerbell,' 'Twinkletoes,' and 'Teensy.' I constantly have people come up to me after I've finished singing and tell me they think I'm a pixie, so I think I must be."

— **Leprechauns:** Sean (not his real name) is a red-haired, red-bearded man with a paunch (he looks like he has a small pillow under his T-shirt—which is usually green). Anyone who sees him would think, *There goes a leprechaun,* because he looks like a six-foot version of a lawn ornament. I call Sean "the Ambassador of Fun" whenever he's at my workshops, because he's a master at making people laugh and smile. Sean's also an accomplished opera singer who often leads my workshops in a round of "Let There Be Peace on Earth" or some other spiritual song.

— **Dolphins:** Gayle loves dolphins, and regularly leads group excursions to swim with them in exotic locations. She even looks like a dolphin, with her sleekly rounded body and oval eyes. Interestingly, Gayle runs a swimming pool company. Her sun sign is Pisces, the sign of the fish, and a water sign. She says, "I love the ocean and *have* to spend time there to recharge. I love dolphins and whales and spend much time in the ocean swimming with them. I asked my guides why I feel so connected to the ocean, and I was told, 'Because, Gayle, you are *of* the ocean.' At first, I didn't understand what that meant. Now I do believe that I may have been a dolphin before."

— **Unicorns:** Brian (not his real name) has a protruding jaw, prominent cheekbones, large eyes, and a chiseled face, like an Arabian horse. Reminiscent of a unicorn's mane, Brian dresses in long, flowing shirts untucked from his pants, and prefers his hair to be on the longer side. If you look closely at Brian, you can see or feel a beautifully braided unicorn horn protruding from his forehead. In psychic readings, clairvoyants tell Brian that his spirit guides are unicorns. This doesn't surprise him, as he has always felt an affiliation for this remarkable beast. In fact, Brian has many items that sport unicorn images. His personality is that of a hunter — he goes after spiritually based opportunities and relationships, and magically manifests new doors opening for himself. Brian says that he knows he's an Incarnated Unicorn—the message was given to him by his own guides and angels long ago.

— **Merangels, Merfairies, and Starmaids:** Incarnated Mermaids are often a mixture of the realms, such as the Merangels (mermaids with angel wings); the Merfairies (mermaids with fairy wings); and the Starmaids (mermaids with Starperson qualities). Incarnated Mermaids watch over the oceans, lakes, rivers, and streams of the world; and also the fish, animals, and birds that live in those locales.

Pamela looks like a beautiful dark-haired mermaid, with the face of an exotic Starperson. I first met her while teaching the Angel

Therapy Practitioner certification course in Florida. The last night of the course, Pamela jumped into the ocean with her clothes on. She looked just like a mermaid as she swam, and even more like one when she walked out of the ocean with her long hair and dress dripping.

Pamela says, "I call myself a 'Starmermaid' because I have traits of both a Starperson and an Elemental. My guides and angels have also confirmed this ancestral mix. My dreams and visions are often filled with images of water and stars or space. As a child, I was always drawn to water, fascinated by it. For me, rooting on the solid earth has always been a problem. On land, my feet and ankles are weak; and I suffer from dry skin, bunions, athletes' foot at times, and even fungus of the toenails. However, when I look up at the stars, I feel a sense of longing."

— **Incarnated Animals:** Barbara considers herself to be an "incarnated cat." She says, "I feel a camaraderie with cats and plants, and my hair has been a sexy silver color since I was a young woman of 20. I'm surrounded by lots of pet cats, and I communicate with felines and plants wonderfully. I don't especially *like* people, but will help when needed as long as they don't infringe on my quiet, private time. I have always been a cat. I worship cats and believe that if the energy in the Universe has some type of form, it would be a wonderful cat-being. Like a cat, I'm able to tell if a person is going to perform evil acts—perhaps not specifically what the acts are, but I can feel at the first meeting if a person has evil or honorable intentions. I want to tell the world that we have to respect one another, the animal-beings, and especially our Earth Mother . . . the environment."

Some of the Incarnated Elementals not described are brownies, sprites (water beings), and tree people (beings with a strong, protective affiliation with trees).

Life-Path Work for Incarnated Elementals

Incarnated Elementals do well in artistic or media-related careers, including music, film, comedy, writing, publishing, dance, and yoga.

Because they tend to be optimistic and are wonderful manifesters, they also make powerful motivational speakers. Incarnated Elementals love an audience and do well teaching groups of people. They also enjoy nature-related jobs, such as pet-sitting or grooming; gardening and nursery work; conservation; and forestry.

Guidance and Suggestions If You're an Incarnated Elemental

— **Spend a lot of time in nature.** As I've emphasized repeatedly in this chapter, it's essential for Incarnated Elementals to be outdoors regularly, regardless of the weather. So, if this is your realm, take off your shoes and stockings and walk on the grass every day as a way of staying grounded and connected to the earth.

— **Laugh and play.** Elementals who don't play often become depressed. So, look for ways to be silly, have fun, and laugh daily.

— **Manifest consciously.** See yourself as healthy, fulfilled, abundant, and loved. Call upon your counterparts in the spiritual Elemental kingdom to help you manifest your desires.

— **Don't throw fireballs.** Elementals' tempers are legendary, and Incarnated Elementals are no exception. When you throw a fit of rage, be careful, because you're literally throwing fireballs of hot emotion! These fireballs can cause the objects of your wrath emotional or physical pain. Your power is like a volcano when you erupt, so please use caution.

— **Engage in environmentalism.** Volunteer your time or give donations to charities involved in cleaning the earth or helping animals. Recycle religiously, and spend the extra money for nontoxic cleaning chemicals and environmentally friendly products.

Chapter 5

Starpeople

Hollywood films and sensationalistic books portray extraterrestrials as vicious warmongers. Yet, to ETs, Earthlings are the ones who are violent—so violent, in fact, that many ETs were asked to take on human bodies to try to avert mass destruction. We call these benevolent helpers *Starpeople* (or, the singular *Starperson*).

Thank God for Starpeople. They came from physical and nonphysical galaxies and took on Earthly lives to spread kindness on an "as needed" basis. Their collective niceness helps to defuse the anger, stress, and rage that could lead to nuclear war. If Earth is destroyed, the negative effects will ripple through many galaxies. The Starperson's assignment, then, is to prevent nuclear war at any cost. The main avenue for this lofty goal is through the expression of kindness and common decency to others—a domino effect of sorts.

On any given day, Starpeople calmly smile as they perform unselfish deeds for those whom they meet. Those whom they help barely notice them, yet Starpeople don't perform acts of service in order to gain accolades. Such deeds are an innate necessity to them—as if some sort of inner programming compels them to act. They aren't concerned that people rarely thank them.

.Starpeople are everywhere that kindness is needed. They are grocery store checkers, postal clerks, bank tellers, and customer service agents. With their wallflower looks and personalities, Starpeople prefer to stay "behind the scenes." Their mission doesn't call for high visibility. Quite the contrary: Starpeople are "undercover do-gooders" who hope no one notices them.

This is the first Earthly life for many Starpeople. And because this planet is so violent, emotionally and physically, Starpeople often feel overwhelmed and wish to return home. After all, Earth is one of the most turbulent planets in the Universe, and, in fact, the Universal powers have us quarantined so that we won't harm other planets. Earth is considered as volatile as a teenager on steroids wielding a loaded gun.

Since it would upset most people to receive intervention from ETs—no matter how benevolent they might be—these mighty and gentle beings elected to take human form and walk among us. On the inside, they're the same as anyone else: beautiful sparks of Divine light made from the same Creator. Yet because they've spent their lifetimes in non-Earthly locales, Starpeople may seem odd in behavior or looks.

Socially awkward due to their inexperience with Earth life, Starpeople may feel rejected by others. Many of the Starpeople interviewed for this book reported a history of being viciously teased in childhood, and sometimes in adulthood as well.

These experiences make the Starperson especially homesick for a planet where they fit in and know the rules of social engagement. Starperson Linda recalls, "When I was a teenager, I used to sit in my front yard and pray for a UFO to come and take me away, to take me home."

In a similar vein, Starperson Scott says, "Metaphorically, I've had my bags packed and have been ready to go home all my life. I'd prefer to work from the other side as a guide. I can remember being on another planet before coming here and being asked to participate in this planet's current drama."

Starpeople often have distinctive physical characteristics that set them apart. Rarely average height, most male Starpeople are tall and thin; with the female Starpeople being small in stature, with either thin or heavyset bodies. Of course, there are exceptions, but in general, the Starpeople's bodies—like their lives—are usually out of the norm in both height or weight.

Starpeople's faces can be long and thin, especially if they have tall, slender bodies. Starpeople who are petite have rounder faces. It appears that the planet-of-origin may influence their specific physical characteristics.

Across the board, Starpeople have unusually shaped and colored eyes. It's common for Starpeople to have crescent moon-shaped eyes, like an inverted U. Their eyes are often gray, green, or black-brown, and seem to glow from within, as if they have bright lights behind them. Starpeople may also have rings of lighter color around their pupils.

Since Starpeople don't like to call attention to themselves, they dress for comfort and practicality, instead of for fashion or show. Female Starpeople wear a minimum of makeup and don't like to fuss with their hair. Even a Starperson surveyed who's a professional hairdresser told me that she doesn't spend much time on her own hair color or style!

Starpeople have paradoxical personalities: On the one hand, they're eager to assist people without being asked. Yet, they also seem guarded and distant and may be perceived as "cold." They're here to be helpful, without needing to get deeply involved in the process of feelings and emotions, which are foreign to them.

No astrological pattern was apparent among the Starpeople surveyed, perhaps because they originated from a wide array of planets. And, interestingly, there aren't as many famous people who are Starpeople because of their love of staying behind the scenes. A Starperson would be more likely to direct a movie than star in it. Yet, Oprah Winfrey and Keanu Reeves are reputed to be Starpeople with high-minded purposes who are using the media as their vehicle to teach. Many believe that the film *The Matrix*, starring Reeves, contained a timely message warning us of technological dependency.

Many Starpeople wonder what their life's purpose is and are relieved to find out that it involves being helpful on an ongoing and nonspecific basis—in other words, to help in whatever way is necessary. There is no one specific "job" or "task" that they need to perform during their lifetimes as long as they're doing their best to transform human frowns into smiles.

Starperson Kath says, "It feels as if I was placed here to be available for helping anyone or anything that needs my assistance. Not a day goes by without someone needing my help in one form or another. It has been frustrating because I've never felt like I had a 'true purpose.'" Kath was relieved to discover that her continual acts of kindness and helpfulness *do*, in fact, represent her purpose.

Connections with Home

Most Starpeople have interests in UFOs, life on other planets, space travel, and ETs. They love the *Star Trek* TV series (both old and new), works of science fiction, and anything else that relates to these themes and topics. They completely relate to the movies *K-Pax* and *Man Facing Southeast*, two films about Starpeople in human bodies who were diagnosed as delusional because they spoke the truth about their non-Earthly origins and were put into mental institutions.

As children, Starpeople find that they have an intuitive understanding of spirituality. Many of them eschew traditional religion because it seems too restrictive compared to their understanding of the vastness of Spirit. Starperson Terry says, "I always thought of God as a Universal Intelligence that is way bigger than what conventional churches made claim to." This wisdom was most likely gained from many lifetimes of high-level awareness and experience.

Many Starpeople recall being, or believe that they were, aboard a spacecraft in this lifetime. Several of the Starpeople surveyed even knew their planet of origin. Of course, this isn't material normally discussed in polite company. Remember that these are very ordinary-looking people who know that they aren't from Earth. They're everyone's next-door neighbors, co-workers, and such, which makes reading their stories even more fascinating. Here are a few of them:

— **MaryKay:** "Through guided visualization, I was taken on a trip to find my home. Jesus came forth as my guide. We went deep into the earth, then all of a sudden, we were up in the sky. We ended up at a really bright star, so bright I that I couldn't see anyone. There, I felt the love I'd been searching for my entire life. When I asked where I was, I immediately heard the word *Sirius* . . . and I had never heard that word, or of that star, before."

— **Linda:** "I've always felt like I came from Pleiades. I don't even know how to spell it. As to why I feel like I come from there, I don't know why. It's just a feeling that I have."

— **Scott:** "I know that I spent my last lifetime on a planet call Zeron. As best I can recall, I tended the forests there. I had a rather large head and was very tall. It was a planet to go rest and relax between lessons. It was very beautiful and green, quite lush. I was having a good time there."

Beings who live on other planets have much longer life expectancies than Earth beings. This is due to physiological differences in their bodies. In addition, they don't undergo the stress, pollution, and toxic diets that create wear-and-tear on Earthly bodies. Actually, many ETs have nonphysical bodies on other planets because that's what's best for their mission at that time. But the main reason why beings on other planets have extended lives is that the longer someone lives, the more can be learned.

So, a lifetime on another planet might equate three or four lifetimes here on Earth. That's why some Starpeople choose to have two or more Earthly lives during their "assignment" here. They're still Starpeople because most of their souls' history has been spent on non-Earthly soil.

When Starpeople undergo a past-life regression, the memories may not be their own. Author and past-life regressionist Dolores Cannon made this remarkable discovery while working with a client named Phil. During regressions, Phil recalled various Earthly lives. Then he remembered being on a planet quite different from Earth.

Through a series of regressions, Dolores found that this was actually Phil's first lifetime on Earth. However, he "borrowed" past-life memories from a sort of spiritual library. These borrowed memories of other Earthly lives helped to insulate and buffer Phil as he adapted to the harsh and dense Earth environment. Without these past-life memories, Earth's violence, competition, and greed would have shocked Phil's system. Dolores writes about Phil and his experiences as a Starperson in her brilliant book, *Keepers of the Garden* (Ozark Mountain Publishers).

Even though many Starpeople feel abandoned by their home planets, as if they were dropped off here on Earth without any say in the matter, they still retain connections to home. It's common for Starpeople to have ETs as their spirit guides. They also have etheric cords reaching to starships. And Starpeople frequently soul-travel to their home planets or starships during dreamtime or meditative sojourns.

Energy Work and Sensitivity

All of the Earth Angel realms report extreme sensitivity to energy from crowds, people, and places. Yet, the Starpeople realm is the most apt to study energy healing and make a career of it. In fact, it's amazing how many Starpeople make a living using their hands, whether through energy work, or via tactile occupations such as landscaping, construction, hair styling, manicuring, massage, and assembly-line work.

Reiki seems to be the number-one choice for

energy healing work among Starpeople. This may be because Reiki energy originated from the Pleiades as a gift to Earth beings. It's interesting that Reiki energy clairvoyantly looks like thin bands of rainbow stripes, and this is also how the auras of Starpeople appear (which are visible on aura photos). They look like poles sticking vertically out of the Starperson's body, like hairs standing on end.

Toward the end of my six-day Angel Therapy Practitioner certification courses, the students gather into groups of their Earth Angel realms. They then spend time together with other realm members, comparing notes about their similarities, and generally bonding with like-minded souls. I'll often interview the realm members to show patterns among them. At my most recent course, every single person from the Starperson realm was also a Reiki master!

Starperson Terry says, "I am super-sensitive to energy. When I do Reiki, I can feel the shift of energy, and it pulls my hands where they should be for releasing the negative energies. Energy feels thick to me, like I'm pushing gum around."

And Starperson Nancy says, "When I do healing work, my hands heat up tremendously. I can feel the heat in a problem area on the person I'm working on."

Starpeople and Relationships

Starpeople may be born to non-Starpeople parents. These parents might not even be from any realm of the Earth Angels. As a result, the family is not able to relate to the Starperson child, and the boy or girl ends up feeling disconnected from the birth family. Starperson Kathy recalls, "As a child, I constantly felt alone and different, even though I had five siblings."

Indeed, most planets don't have the birth and family systems of Earth life. Elsewhere, it's common for beings to be birthed in laboratories, à la the "test-tube baby" process. The emotional bonding that occurs in families here on Earth is alien to other planets as well. This is one reason why Starpeople may be perceived as friendly but distant. They're helpful, yet there's a certain degree of underlying coldness that's evident if someone attempts to create a close bond. And no wonder: Starpeople are task oriented, not relationship oriented. They have a job to do, and they aren't geared toward making relationships their top priority.

Starperson Scott says, "Realizing that I was a Starperson was a validation that has helped me to accept some of my colder traits, and the distance I sometimes feel toward others."

Starperson Terry has had a similar realization: "I'm different in a way that many don't understand. I feel like an outsider and very much of a loner. Most of the time, I'd rather be alone than with a group of people and their issues."

Being with other Starpeople is a way to feel accepted. Linda says, "My husband is a Starperson like me, and because of this, we connect 100 percent."

Linda's husband is 12 years younger than she is, and it seems that many female Starpeople have relationships with younger men. Typically, female Starpeople say, "I know that this man is from my home planet." Sometimes this age difference interferes with building a fully committed love relationship. It seems that male Starpeople may have come to Earth several years after the females.

When Starpeople do marry, they have very few children. Many Starpeople skip having children altogether. Linda says, "I'm 50 years old and have had a hysterectomy, so I won't be having any children. I always knew I wouldn't have kids—actually, I just didn't care either way. If my husband wanted some, fine. If he didn't, that was okay, too. But somehow I just *knew* I wouldn't bear children."

Starperson Terry says that she's never been interested in what she calls "conventional family dynamics."

Starpeople often have C-section births. Perhaps that's because on other planets, vaginal births are unheard of, since babies are "bred" in laboratories. In fact, many planets' inhabitants are androgynous, without clear gender distinctions. Extraterrestrial babies aren't created through the Earthly methods of sexual intercourse, sperm, and eggs, but through a transfer of energies and the intention to create—a method portrayed in the movie *Cocoon*.

Starpeople may have made a "contract" to *not* get married or have children while living an Earth life. They probably had no prior experiences with family and love relationships and didn't even think to put marriage and children into their Earth-life contract! Having a family may interfere with the Starperson's mission, and create karma that could keep them mired in Earth's reincarnation cycles.

Also, this may be the first lifetime that a Starperson has a clear-cut gender. The female may feel uncomfortable in her woman's body, and the male may feel like an awkward imposter posing as a man. Yet, when Starpeople get to Earth and see happy couples walking arm-in-arm, they may wish to share in that experience. Some Starpeople are able to manifest marriage and family, while others find that this type of union perpetually eludes them.

Handling Earth Life

As mentioned earlier, Starpeople are extra-sensitive to violence. All of the Earth Angel realms report an aversion toward violence and conflict. However, of all the realms, Starpeople seem to be the most repulsed by fighting in any form. Linda says, "I can't tolerate violence in the least. I can't stand it when people even raise their voices. It's almost unbearable for me. It usually brings me to tears when someone scolds me." Most Starpeople surveyed told me that they don't watch, listen to, or read the news because it upsets them too much.

The Starpeople see an eventual end to violence . . . if peace-loving men and women will take a stance in the form of prayer or guided action. In the meantime, Starpeople stay faithfully at their Earthly posts, being nice guys and gals in everyday situations. Yet, deep down, they're homesick for the peaceful life they once knew in a faraway place.

Starpeople who have learned how to handle Earth life say that it helps to connect with others in their realm. They're not difficult to spot if you look for their telltale physical characteristics. Or, you can be sure to find them near the ocean. Every single Starperson surveyed said that living near water, especially the ocean, was a *must*.

MaryKay explains this connection with Starpeople and water: "I realized that I need to live near a body of water to get balanced. I go there to feel the power of this huge body of water and the waves, and it's like a battery recharge for me." And, of course, Starpeople tend to frequent UFO conventions and science fiction study groups.

Here are some other comments from Starpeople:

— **Starperson Linda says:** "My advice to other Starpeople is that it's okay to feel like you don't belong here on Earth . . . because you don't. Just be comfortable with this fact. You're special because you came here to assist this planet with accomplishing peace. You're on this planet by choice, to heal."

— **And Scott's advice for Starpeople is:**
"Find others to connect with who share your common view, and keep smiling at all the insanity you're surrounded with. Teach tolerance and patience and especially love, because that's all there really is. And remember, this is only a temporary assignment!"

Life-Path Work for Starpeople

Starpeople are multitaskers and may not settle on one particular career as their life's mission. They may, instead, dabble with several careers consecutively or simultaneously. Starpeople make wonderful Reiki masters, energy healers, massage therapists, chiropractors, and physical therapists. They also enjoy research, engineering, and support staff work. However, the Starpeople must believe in the goals of the company they work for or they'll be miserable in their jobs. Starpeople are kind, hardworking, and efficient, yet wrongly perceived as being aloof or cold. They also prefer to be behind the scenes. Therefore, they're better off doing solo work than being a spokesperson or a front-office employee.

Guidance and Suggestions If You're a Starperson

— **Know that small acts of kindness *do* count.** As a Starperson, you probably worry about Earth's future, or whether you're doing "enough." You'll feel better by remembering that the thousands of seemingly small acts of kindness you do add up to a huge contribution toward creating a peaceful planet.

— **Seek out other Starpeople.** It's essential to be around like-minded folks. If you hold the intention of meeting other Starpeople, you'll soon easily attract them into your life.

— **Appreciate your uniqueness.** Your natural inclinations run counter to many Earthlings. Your standard of beauty is based more on what's on the inside than the outside—the opposite of many humans. Your priorities are more task oriented than relationship focused. So, Starperson, please honor your uniqueness, stand firm in your beliefs, and don't water down your capabilities by trying to conform.

Chapter 6

Walk-Ins

A Walk-In is a soul who bypasses the usual process of acquiring a human body through being born, going to grade school, and so forth. Instead, the soul makes an agreement with another soul to make an exchange of life energy at some point. What usually happens is that the Walk-In soul approaches a human who's depressed about their Earthly life. The Walk-In soul begins negotiating during the human's dreamtime, saying, "Instead of your dying or committing suicide, which is a waste of a human body that could be used in service of the Light, please allow me to help. When you're ready, I'll take over your body, and you can go home to heaven with full honors. I'll feed your cat, help your children with their homework, call your mother every Sunday, and take care of your other responsibilities."

So, in essence, Walk-Ins are those who:

- wake up one day and feel like their life is a bad dream, or one they don't recognize;

- don't remember their childhoods or significant chunks of their lives;

- have a history of suicidal fantasies or attempts;

- have heard from friends and family, "You're not the same person anymore!"; and

- make sudden and drastic changes, such as changing their first name, moving, divorcing, switching careers, adopting different religious beliefs, and so on.

"I watched myself plop into this body, and saw the other being wearily leaning into the angel that had come to escort her away," recalls Annette about her Walk-In experience. Annette is no half-wit prone to flights of fancy: She holds a master's degree in education, is the CEO of a natural-care products company, and is also a former director of several large firms. No one would guess by looking at or talking to her that she's a Walk-In.

The Walk-In process is very different from spirit possession, in which a second soul is attached to the person's body and soul. In a Walk-In situation, souls exchange life energy in the same manner that a car is sold to a new owner. Only one soul occupies a Walk-In's body. The soul that leaves is called a "Walk-Out." Since there are more souls desiring a human body than there are bodies to house them, the Walk-In soul may come from a waiting list. Or, Walk-In souls could be "twin flames" or "braided" soulmates of the Walk-Out souls, which means they contracted with the Walk-Out prior to their body's conception. Usually, though, the Walk-In soul is from a high spiritual level, with a purpose requiring immediate access to an adult body to fulfill that mission.

Usually, the souls spend a lot of time discussing their possible soul exchange. They make trial runs, where the Walk-In soul test-drives the new body, and the Walk-Out soul experiences being free of a body. Both parties must be in total agreement before the final exchange is made. This is similar to the process that a person goes through before having a sex-change operation. Since the Walk-In procedure cannot be cancelled (unless prior arrangements are made), both parties have to make sure that they truly want this exchange to occur.

If the decision is made to go ahead, then an "intersection episode" is set. This means that the Walk-Out soul engages in a suicide attempt, an accident, surgery, or an out-of-body experience. Or, the exchange happens while the person is sleeping, napping, or meditating. During the exchange, the old soul leaves and goes to the afterlife plane—exactly as if he or she had died. The new soul immediately enters the body and takes over.

When the new soul awakens, there's usually no memory of the Walk-In process. An amnesia effect occurs whenever a spirit travels from the fourth dimension of the spirit world (where time isn't measured) and lands in the third dimension of Earthly time and life. This is similar to having a soul-travel dream and learning profound information, but being unable to recall any specific information the next morning. The measurement of time here on Earth "flattens" the truths we learn in the spirit plane, because they don't make sense in this environment. Yet, the information is still there in the recesses of the mind, helping and guiding us whether or not we consciously remember it.

So, Walk-In souls don't remember these

exchanges clearly. All they know is that their lives suddenly don't make sense. Out of the blue (as opposed to feeling gradual dissatisfaction), they feel as if they're living in the wrong movie. They don't recognize their children, spouse, or friends. They feel like aliens in their own life.

The Walk-In's family members and friends will say, "You're not the same person!" They may say this as a compliment, or as a complaint. When the Walk-In tries to recall their childhood or recent history, their memories are fuzzy or nonexistent.

They don't relate to their first name, so they change it. This feels better, and encourages them to make other changes that suit their new outlook. They might move, switch occupations, let go of certain people in their life, or initiate a new major project.

The Walk-In soul has a high-level mission to complete and is using the new vehicle (the body) to make that mission happen.

←✳→

The above is what typically happens during a Walk-In soul exchange. As with any situation, there are exceptions. Because this is such a diverse group of souls coming and going, there are no clear patterns among them in terms of physical characteristics, health conditions, or astrological signs. The Walk-In procedure is a process, rather than a realm. Additionally, Walk-In bodies and souls can come from any of the realms. So, for example, a person could have the body of an Incarnated Angel and the soul of a Starperson.

Here are some stories of people who know that they experienced a Walk-In soul exchange:

Sandra

In 1985, Sandra wanted to die. Her two teenage sons were in drug rehab, and she felt so alone as she tried to cope with this crisis. Her soul cried out for help, and her call was answered by a high-level being who offered to take her place and allow Sandra to go "home." Sandra willingly accepted this offer, although it was done unconsciously. She was unaware of it until she underwent extensive hypnosis several years later.

Once Sandra's soul made the swap agreement with the other soul, it occurred during her sleep time. Sandra says, "I woke up one morning, and upon seeing my husband lying beside me, I realized that I had no feeling for him. I wondered, *What is he doing in my bed?* Things just seemed different, and it didn't make sense. One day I was totally head-over-heels in love with my husband, and the next day—nothing! No feelings at all for him."

Sandra felt confused about this and other parts of her life, which also seemed senseless, so she consulted a counselor for a year but still couldn't regain her marital bliss or lose her off-kilter feelings.

Not only had Sandra's feelings changed, but so had her personality and physical features. Overnight, her eyes had changed from brown to hazel, with a new gray ring around the pupil. Amazingly, her shoe size changed from a six to a seven-and-a-half. Sandra was formerly introverted and kept her feelings to herself. Now she was vivacious and loudly opinionated.

What was going on?! Sandra demanded to know.

The Universe provides answers to our questions, and soon after, Sandra met an intuitive woman who became her friend over the next 12 years. One day, the woman told Sandra, "I think you're a Walk-In," and taught her all about that concept and why she believed Sandra was one.

Sandra says, "I know that Spirit brought her to me to guide and help me. Once I found out that I was a Walk-In, everything that was confused in my life fell into place, and I became very peaceful. I felt in the depths of my soul that it was true, even though I had never heard

the term before. This knowledge helped me
feel more at ease, and more comfortable about
being here."

The woman took Sandra to a hypnotherapist,
who helped Sandra remember her Walk-In
process through a series of regressions. Sandra
discovered that her new soul wasn't from Earth
at all, but was an androgynous being from the
star system Cygnus (also known as the "swan
constellation").

Like Sandra, many of the people whom I've
surveyed about Walk-In experiences say that their
soul has extraterrestrial origins. These Starpeople
souls come to Earth for the important mission of
bypassing our possible future into nuclear war. Yet,
they also bypass the human birth process and incarnate into adult bodies when the original soul agrees
to vacate and "walk out." We would call such souls
a "Walk-In Starperson." Karen, who directs a spiritual healing center in New Jersey, is a perfect
example:

Karen

"I *knew* my home wasn't here on Earth, so
one day I asked the angels to explain my origins in a dream. I asked that they wake me up
after the explanation so that I would remember

everything. That night, I dreamed that I was talking to a man with a long ponytail. He told me that he was going to teach me how to pray, and asked me to raise my hands to the sky and recite the Lord's Prayer. I began with, 'Our Father, who art in heaven,' with my hands extended toward heaven. Suddenly, my whole body felt like it got zapped with this strong energy, like I'd stuck a pin into an electrical outlet.

"I said to the man, 'Oh my God, you're not from here, are you?' He said, 'No, I'm not! I'm from where you're from.' I then asked, 'And where is that?' He replied, 'Andromeda!' And then my dog started throwing up, which woke me up. I felt as if a weight had been lifted off my shoulders, because I finally remembered where I was from, as well as my soul's purpose."

Mir'iam (formerly Shirley)

In 1973, Shirley was very ill and had consulted many doctors trying to discover why she had so much pain in her abdomen. A doctor in Dayton, Ohio, finally decided to hospitalize her and conduct exploratory surgery. In the hospital, Shirley was in excruciating pain while awaiting her surgery.

She recalls, "I was tired of life, tired of my family situation where I felt burdened and alone, and tired of my painful body. Aloud in my hospital bed, I asked God to take me from this earth if my life couldn't change. I was truly ready. Then I dozed, and either dreamed or experienced looking at my frail gray body lying on the bed."

Shirley doesn't remember anything more about the next three days prior to her surgery. Although she had a major operation, Shirley returned home within a week. Three days after that, she returned to work, to the surprise of her doctors. Her recovery was remarkable, and Shirley was filled with amazingly high levels of energy. Shirley also noticed that she was highly psychic. Several people, including her boss, commented that she seemed like a totally different person. Their remarks about the changes in her were generally positive.

She even changed her name to 'Mir,' and later added "I am" to the end of her name, to create, "Mir'iam." She was happy with her new name and new outlook. Yet, her husband complained, "I want my old-fashioned girl back!" Unhappy with her marital and family relationships, Shirley started undergoing personal counseling.

One day, she felt exhausted and decided to lie down. During a three-hour period of contemplation and rest, Mir'iam reexperienced the scene at the Dayton Ohio Hospital. She realized that the unaccounted-for three days prior to her surgery was when the Walk-In soul exchange occurred.

The pieces of the puzzle are still fitting together for Mir'iam, including the origins of the soul that now inhabits her body—the soul that is now *her*. Mir'iam says, "For a while now, I've known that I came from a planet yet unknown or identified, and that it had an indigo hue. I decided to view pictures of the planets on a daily basis, and I had a very strong reaction when I saw the cluster of stars within the Pleiades. Does this mean that the Seven Sisters and the stars in that constellation are my home? I realize at this point that I've known that place before in some incarnation and loved it, and that it doesn't necessarily mean it's the planet from which I originated in this soul experience."

Annette

"I've chosen to use the term 'Walk-In' for myself because it most accurately describes my experiences of great life changes," says Annette, whom you met at the beginning of this chapter. "I'm also careful not to cling too closely to any term or story, especially in light of our limited third-dimensional consciousness. Yet, my life is now distinctly different. *I'm* different, since the Walk-Out experience. Life's deep angst—the worry and the heaviness—are gone now. I feel lighter, younger, and refreshed. Life is doable, without all the roar and moans of my former victim's energy.

"I'm still acclimating, and my memory, task, and work abilities are suffering. But I don't seem to care much. I feel it will all come together. So much resistance is gone. Most of my dreams are just out of touch, as if they're happening in a different language I haven't learned yet. People ask me, 'Wow, what happened to you? You look ten years younger!' and some people don't recognize me at first, seeming a bit floored when they do. I'm so much more open now. I've learned that bliss is a choice."

Barbara

"Ever since my attempted suicide, I don't remember much about my younger years. It all happened in November 1986. Life wasn't good, as I had just ended another bad relationship that seemed like the straw that broke the camel's back. I decided to kill myself and jump off a bridge. Well, I sat on that wall on the highway overpass and just couldn't do it. I went there three days in a row, and each time, I felt a power push me back, a power so great that it kept me from committing suicide.

"Yet I was determined to end my pain in this way. So, I took my car and drove it into a telephone pole. But instead of killing myself, I felt someone or something pull the steering wheel back and prevent the suicide." Barbara believes that this "someone or something" is the Walk-In soul who is the current soul inhabiting her body today.

Ken

"As a young man, I was very unhappy. I felt that there was no way out of my depression. One morning, I'd fully given up on life. I begged God for help. Life wasn't for me anymore—not the way I was living it. Spiritual thinking and ideas hadn't yet presented themselves to me.

"Yet something started talking to me. Not something physical, though. I didn't know anything about spirits. I just thought at that moment that I was plain crazy. All I could do to calm myself down was pray to God. As I prayed, a voice said loudly in my mind: *You have a choice right now. Do you want to live?* I replied, 'If my life is to be lived like this, then I don't want to live anymore.'

"After that day, I seemed to have a new drive and motivation. *Something* was with me, watching over me, helping me. White and colored lights began to appear around me, and things started to move and fly across the room. At first, this terrified me, and I thought I was hallucinating. But then I realized that these things weren't hurting me, and I developed a good feeling toward them.

"Yet I still didn't want to live. Years later, I was in my room, doing some hard thinking. I was ready to go. My choice was made: I didn't want to live anymore. That's when I saw all these lights come into the room, and I was terrified! I could feel them touching me like human hands and fingers on my body, with extreme grace and subtlety. Only the sensation of a higher vibration was present. I asked the lights to leave if they were not of God, and they didn't. So, I began to trust them, and I allowed the lights to touch me on my head and back. I could feel that they were good and loving.

"For the first time in my life, I felt an incredible love and warmth as something came into my body at the same time that the old self left. I now know that those lights were angels. They helped me feel so comfortable, strong, and different. Suddenly, the entire left side of my body started to feel like pins and needles, like when your foot falls asleep. The left side of my face and body felt like rubber and remained that way for the next three days.

"After that, I handled situations in a new, confident way. Today I'm a new man, and I thank God for this change. After my Walk-In experience, things were never the same. I'd had a long history of battling depression, which changed drastically after my Walk-In experience. I'm no longer on medication, and I've never been happier!"

Memories

If you can't decide if you're a Walk-In, ask yourself, "Are there parts of my childhood, or significant chunks of my life, that I just can't remember?" If the answer is yes, then you might very well be a Walk-In. On the other hand, if you *can* clearly remember your childhood and most of your life, then while you may be from another realm and may have had significant spiritual experiences—they probably didn't involve a soul exchange.

Life-Path Work for Walk-Ins

If you're a Walk-In, you came to Earth to teach about Divine Love and peace, and the form that this teaching takes is secondary to the mission. You may feel an urgency to get on with your mission, and it's a mistake to delay it while awaiting a "perfect" way to express your teaching work. Similarly, don't delay teaching until you feel adequately prepared. Such a day may never come, so just jump in and start doing it.

Your teaching begins with modeling peaceful-ness, so a daily morning meditation is a must. No matter what your day job is, use whatever methods you can to be a role model for peace. Ask your guides and angels for opportunities to teach peace on a formal basis, and then walk through the doors as they open for you in response to these prayers. It's not important whether you're famous, wealthy, degreed, published or otherwise—what matters is that you disseminate the concept of peace in what-ever fashion you can, without delay.

Guidance and Suggestions If You're a Walk-In:

— **Know that one person can make a huge difference.** Your soul came here with high expectations and a lofty mission, so you might feel a little blocked or discouraged as you try to make the world a better place. Start with the basics, and know that you can help with small increments and steps, such as making a dona-tion to charity, smiling at those on your path, writing an encouraging letter, or leading a book-study group. Anything you do with the intention of helping counts.

— **Let your light shine.** Although you feel different, you're definitely not inferior, nor are you superior. What you are is a powerful soul with a clear intention to help the world. Don't be afraid to "come out of the spiritual closet" and take a stand, make noise, and help fix the situations that need healing in this world.

— **Make changes as necessary.** If your first name, job, or family situation seems foreign to you, it may be because the previous soul (the Walk-Out) chose them. You don't have to live with these choices! Pray and meditate about your desires, and take guided action toward creating a life that mirrors who you truly are.

‡✻‡

Chapter 7

**The Wise Ones: Reincarnated
Sorceresses, High-Priestesses,
Sorcerers, Wizards, Shamans,
and Witches**

Intense. Exotic. Eccentric. The Wise Ones glow
from the inside. They look like romance-novel
characters, usually with long, silky hair; oval faces;
and haunting eyes complete with a lifetime of shad-
ows beneath them. Earth Angels from this realm
possess profound wisdom and are highly intuitive.
Their eyes are penetrating, and there's no point in
pretending or lying to Wise Ones, because truth is
apparent to them. Eccentric and flamboyant, Wise
Ones love to dress in flowing garments reminiscent
of romantic eras in the past. There's a certain element of mystery accompanying each member of
this realm. It's obvious, when first meeting the gaze
of Wise Ones, that they *know*.

The Wise Ones are humans with past lives in

which they learned how to channel their power into miraculous healings and manifestations, including the ability to affect the weather and material objects (through levitation and telekinesis, and so on). These are the extremely powerful and well-trained magicians of the human race who were called out of "retirement" from the spirit world in order to come back to Earth for the currently urgent situation on our planet.

Their energy is darker and heavier than the other Earth Angel realms. Wise Ones have a somber, serious, almost depressed energy, and they're sometimes quite stern. In relationships, they're highly opinionated in a helpful way. They're the "stage moms" and directors of their friends and family members, always knowing the best route for others to take. If someone wants solid advice, they should ask a Wise One.

Whereas the other realms are new to being human (or have past lives where they were Incarnated Angels, Elementals, and so on), the Wise Ones have been human for eons. Like the other Earth Angels, they feel "different." In fact, some Wise Ones proclaim, "I *am* different, and proud of it!" As one Incarnated Sorcerer put it: "In childhood, I realized I was different and didn't fit in, and that created difficulty—until I finally realized that my uniqueness was a benefit. I wasn't part of the mass or the norm, and when I matured, I realized that this was positive."

For that reason, the Wise Ones are more comfortable with Earth life than those in other realms. They're realistic, compassionate, and patient with people, and they've learned to enjoy their time here. Incarnated Sorceress Linda spoke for many Wise Ones when she said, "I know I'm different from other people, but I don't really feel like an outsider because I basically don't care if most people like me or not." This detachment from other people's opinions is a hallmark of Wise Ones.

The History of the Wise Ones

The common denominator of Wise Ones is the number of years they've logged learning to harness their magical powers. Some developed their own interest in metaphysics, and others were handpicked as children and schooled in the psychic arts. The Wise Ones have lived as High-Priests and Priestesses in Atlantis, Ancient Greece, and Egypt; during Arthurian times; among the Mayans; as

Essenes; and as native medicine men and women. They've witnessed civilizations destroyed, and people murdered for their spiritual beliefs. The Wise Ones know and appreciate the innate darkness within the human ego, but they have an even greater appreciation and respect for the heights to which humans are capable. And this is what they've come back to teach.

On the other side, many Wise Ones were comfortably enjoying the afterlife plane. They'd created paradise-like communities in the spirit world, complete with castles, gardens, and waterfalls. Everything seemed wonderful. But then the Wise Ones were approached by a committee of guides that was trying to enlist retired "spiritual soldiers" back into service. They asked the Wise Ones to return to Earth to teach and model peacefulness, and to remind people how to use their inner power and strength to create harmony.

Some Wise Ones reluctantly agreed to return to Earth. When they got here, they felt the heavy density of the shifting energy. A few Wise Ones, unable to handle this climate, exited immediately by willing their own deaths. Other Wise Ones relegated themselves to an Earth life, but felt depressed or angry about it.

The best-adjusted Wise Ones were those who resumed the study of Earth-based spirituality—such as astrology, Wicca, kabbalistic magic, paganism, rituals, crystal healing, herbology, candle invocations, shamanism, and so forth.

Grethel says one of the reasons why she believes she is a Reincarnated Sorceress is "because of my early interest in chants, herbs, magic wands, the apparatus of ritual (candles, incense, water, and so on). I also had an 'imaginary friend' as a child who was a wizard. If that weren't enough, my great aunt called me a 'sorceress' when I was young."

Members of the Wise Ones realm have spent lifetimes developing their spiritual and magical gifts. They're well practiced in the spiritual arts of manifestation, alchemy, and healing. They're born as psychic children who may view their gifts as being curses, especially if they're prescient about a forthcoming "negative" situation. The children may blame themselves for not diverting a tragedy, since they foresaw it. Yet, these psychic insights are often an opportunity for the individuals to pray about it. If they were supposed to intervene, they would have been clearly told what to do to prevent the situation.

The majority of Wise Ones whom I interviewed had vivid memories of past lives where they were witches, wizards, priests, and the like. Most of the Wise Ones surveyed had strong emotional reactions to the era of "witch burnings" from the years 1300 to 1700. Many of them have full, or fragmented, memories of being burned, hung, or otherwise killed for their spiritual differences. Sara, for example, says, "I have memories of being burned at the stake while people screamed and cursed at me. I remember being viciously tortured."

The "Witch-Burning Craze" consisted of a mass superstition that anything bad—whether spoiled crops or sick children—was caused by a witch's spells. It was decided that the only way to purge this "evil" was through the burning of the witch's blood. Many of the witches were hunted by their neighbors, local governments, and churches. In more humane situations, they were killed before being tied to a pole and set on fire. Yet, in France, Germany, and Switzerland, most witches were burned alive.

Even those who weren't actually killed have conscious memories of this time period. They remember being afraid of the Inquisition, the Knights Templar, the Cathar trials (the Cathars were a pagan group in 13th-century Europe who were targeted by Pope Innocent III and were hunted and put to death), and the other various ways in which the witch-hunts manifested. The threat of death hung over everyone during those times, and the memory makes Wise Ones nervous about fully reopening their spiritual gifts.

As a result, many Wise Ones hold back from unleashing their great power because of these ancient memories! Yet, the reason why they've elected to be here at this time is to teach and use those spiritual tools. A Wise One's purpose involves dusting off their psychic and spiritual healing abilities. And since we can only feel happy and fulfilled if we're engaged in our purpose, then it's necessary for Wise Ones to open and redevelop their spiritual gifts.

The Wise Ones have a special affinity with the Elemental kingdom and vice versa. Not only do fairies and elves play a role in Earth-based spiritual practices, but deep friendships were forged between the Elementals and the Wise Ones. In ancient times, people recognized the benefits of working with the Elemental kingdom, yet the churches felt threatened by this power outside of their walls. So, a negative public relations campaign against fairies, elves, and other Elementals was waged. To this day, many people are afraid of the beautiful Elementals.

Because the Elementals were so tied in with the Wise Ones in ancient and modern times, some Incarnated Elementals may believe that they're actually from the Wise Ones realm. That's due to the shared experiences and memories of these two realms. So, a female Incarnated Elemental may remember the witch burnings—not because she was burned, but because she witnessed her Wise Ones friends being burned. She may be confused and think that these are *her* memories of being burned.

Yet, the differences between the two realms are clear: Wise Ones are more solemn, dark, and serious than the playful, mischievous Incarnated Elementals. Wise Ones have long, oval faces and prefer to wear their hair long, too (even if they currently have it cut short for business reasons); while Incarnated Elementals have round faces, and often wear their hair short (except in the case of Incarnated Fairies and Mermaids). Male Wise Ones often wear their hair in ponytails or combed back with gel. Actors Della Reese, Angelica Huston, Jack Nicholson, and Jimmy Smits are examples of the looks and intensity of the Wise Ones realm.

The Wise Ones may dress eccentrically or romantically, reflecting their favorite past-life period. Female Wise Ones prefer long, flowy "goddess gowns" in dark colors, with chunky crystal necklaces. Male Wise Ones favor woven shirts in natural fabrics or Renaissance-style shirts. The men may wear spiritually significant pendant necklaces, such as Celtic crosses or Ohm insignias. Wise Ones often love to attend Renaissance Fairs in full costume, where they can relive the highs and lows of their past lives.

The Wise Ones have dragons, wizards, and goddesses as spirit guides. They're very interested in the study of ancient eras that may be regarded as mythical, such as Avalon, Atlantis, and Lemuria. They collect wizard statues, and love books and movies dealing with magical themes, such as *The Lord of the Rings* series, the *Harry Potter* books, and anything related to Arthurian times. Many Wise Ones are also history buffs.

As Incarnated High-Priestess Marlies wrote, "I love Greek and Egyptian mythology. I can easily relate to Isis in the Egyptian tradition, and I love Pallas Athena—the goddess of wisdom and war. I deeply love her stories and her support she gave to Ulysses. With great passion, I studied ancient

Greek, and I relate to all the goddesses of Olympus."

Wise Ones are also highly sensitive to moon phases—physically and emotionally affected by the full- and new-moon cycles. They often engage in "full-moon ceremonies" and celebrate the equinoxes.

Patterns Among the Wise Ones

No clear-cut astrological pattern was apparent among the Wise Ones interviewed for this book. Interestingly, though, every Wise One surveyed knew their sun, moon, rising, and ascendant astrological signs. This was in sharp contrast to members surveyed from other realms, who often didn't even know their sun sign, and rarely knew their moon sign. Clearly, the Wise Ones are knowledgeable about astrology and appreciative of its applications.

A high percentage of the Wise Ones surveyed had a past or current history of heart and cardiovascular health conditions. Mitral valve prolapse, high blood pressure, tachycardia, arrhythmia, heart murmurs, and heart attacks were rampant among this realm. Could this be from heartache within the realm, for loving Earth and her people so much, and watching its potential destruction? Or, is it residual pain from the witch-hunts, where the Wise Ones' blood was burned and their hearts impaled with stakes?

Louise Hay says in *Heal Your Body* that the metaphysical meaning behind heart problems is "long-standing emotional problems." The Wise Ones have carried emotional pain for eons from their many Earthly lives—talk about long-standing! Other reasons for heart problems, according to Louise, include "lack of joy, hardening of the heart, and belief in strain and stress."

The Wise Ones whom I've met are intense individuals and hardworking teachers. They teach without ceasing, often by giving brief but deeply philosophical advice to people. Yet, the look in many Wise Ones' eyes reveals years of disappointment in their students. A Wise One recently told me, "If people would just take my advice, all of their problems would cease to be. I'm not being arrogant—I *just know* what would help them. Yet, most people ignore the advice and keep wallowing in their troubles."

Since the Wise Ones' purpose is to teach and be way-showers, perhaps this frustration with their mission is their greatest heartbreak.

The Wise Ones in Relationships

Most Wise Ones long for a magical and mystical soulmate marriage. They may feel the elusive presence of a kindred soul whom they've known for many lifetimes. This leads to a search for the Beloved, and until he or she is found, the Wise One may choose to be romantically alone. Or worse, the Wise One may try settling for an unfulfilling relationship.

In previous lives, Wise Ones may have taken vows of chastity or celibacy. These unbroken vows can follow someone into a current life and wreak havoc. Wise One Audrey is a perfect example. She knew she'd had past lives as a witch and also as a nun. As a witch, she was involved with pagan rituals, celebrating the earth, nature, and the human body. This often involved ceremonies with nudity and sexuality. The reigning powers at the time deemed this material focus to be heretical, and she was burned at the stake. In her next life, Audrey was a nun, where she took a vow of celibacy. Still, she retained her mystical interests and abilities. In her present-day life, Audrey continued to practice spell-castings, and knew how to manifest very well. However, her sex life was stunted in a sexless relationship with an impotent husband who was too proud to take medication or get sexual counseling. We "broke" her vows of celibacy, and she was able to rekindle her sexuality.

So, Wise Ones do best in their love lives when they use their remarkable magical powers to manifest the love they seek. Even if their true Beloved is not currently incarnate and is in the spirit world between lives, Wise Ones can manifest wonderfully fulfilling love relationships with the power of their focused intentions.

Wise Ones do best when they have friends whom they respect and admire. Otherwise, the Wise One may have friends who are actually "clients." These "friendships" are one-sided, with the Wise One acting as teacher, and the friend acting as student. The Wise Ones never get a chance to discuss their own troubles because they're cast in the strong, empowered role.

Wise Ones are often accused of being know-it-alls. This accusation actually has a kernel of truth to it, because Wise Ones are tapped into the all-knowing collective unconscious. They're also highly psychic. Linda, a Reincarnated Sorceress says, "Most often, I know what people are about to say. They get irritated with me because I finish their sentences."

The Wise Ones' children may accuse them of being controlling parents—again, because of this realm's compulsion to teach. Wise Ones *can't not* teach; however, they can temper their instruction so that it's more palatable. Instead of lecturing, for example, they can create a teaching experience that's entertaining and instructive.

As with their love lives, it's important for Wise Ones to use conscious visualizations of happy, healthy relationships with friends and family. They can use that remarkable power to see themselves surrounded by strong and loving friends who help *them*.

So if you think you're a Wise One, see and feel your children appreciating your teachings. Don't worry about how these manifestations will come about. Just know that they will. And then release the visions to the Universe so that they can manifest quickly and easily.

Magical Wise Ones

If you're a Wise One, you're a highly trained magician, and if some part of your life isn't working right now, take a proactive role in healing this area. If you passively wait for the Universe to direct you,

you may find yourself spinning your wheels and going nowhere. That's because Wise Ones such as yourself are co-creators, and the Universe prefers to await your wishes and to fulfill them as asked. However, Wise Ones know from experience that not everything asked for leads to happiness. For this reason, it's prudent to pray or ask for guidance *to know what to ask for.*

Faith in these abilities is crucial, even if it's just 5 or 10 percent faith. If you ask for something but harbor the fear that it might not happen, you'll block the manifestation. If you need to, you can "borrow" faith from one of your guides. Or, you can ask the Universe to clear away fears that are thwarting your full faith.

You may have, like many other Wise Ones, taken vows in your past lives as a spiritual aspirant or devotee (such as a nun or a monk). Among the most common are vows of suffering, self-sacrifice or retribution, poverty, chastity, virginity, celibacy, obedience, and silence. Unless these vows are severed, they can follow you to Earth and place barriers in your love and sexual areas, finances, and life in general. No one is truly free until these past-life vows are broken. The only healthy vows are those that *you* decide upon—the ones you make with yourself. Even then, you'll want to regularly review them to see if they're still valid.

Break these vows and their effects by strongly affirming:

> *"I hereby sever any vows of*
> *suffering, self-sacrifice, or*
> *retribution that I may have made,*
> *in all directions of time.*
> *I rescind any negative effects of*
> *these vows, now and forever."*

Then, repeat this phrase for other vows (poverty, celibacy, and so on). Since these vows often involved signing a document with your own blood, you'll need to break the vow with an even greater amount of power. It's especially powerful to light a black candle (which always help us to release negativity and break up stagnant situations) and conduct the ceremony during a full moon, which is the time of releasement. Then, stand up, and stamp your foot down strongly as you make each statement aloud. Really say it like you mean it when you sever those vows!

←✳→

Wise Ones, always remember the power of the word. Become clear about what you desire, and then command—through words—that it happen. You are a master spell-caster, both in the name of your fears *and* your heart's desires. So you just as easily create self-fulfilling prophecies in the direction of your ego's dictates as well as your higher self. Command your ego to silence, and direct your higher self to increase the volume of its voice.

As your manifestations appear in tangible form, welcome them with open arms. Wise Ones sometimes push away manifestations for fear they don't deserve them. Remember, though, that these manifestations are tools that help your teaching and healing practice. Your students and clients deserve to be helped by a Wise One whose material needs are met. Put all scarcity or vows of suffering behind you now, Wise One.

Life-Path Work for Wise Ones

As a Wise One, you're a natural-born leader who's respected because of your charisma, your air of confidence, the way that you carry yourself, and your personal power. People naturally respect and admire you; they're even intimidated by you. So they feel comfortable following your lead.

Due to your many lifetimes of spiritual learning and teaching, you'd probably enjoy a career as a spiritual teacher, astrologer, psychic, spiritual healer, channeler, or oracle card reader. Most Wise Ones don't do well as employees or followers, unless you respect your boss or leader. You would make an excellent company president or entrepreneur, especially with your organizational skills combined with your intuitive knowledge of how to improve situations.

However, you, like most Wise Ones, would feel frustrated working with unmotivated audiences or clients who won't take your advice.

Guidance and Suggestions If You're a Wise One

— **Honor the power of the word.** Use vigilance with your thoughts and words to ensure that they mirror what you want, not what you fear. You manifest so quickly that you can't afford to think or talk about your fears. Focus all your energies on manifesting your desires and life purpose.

— **Honor your past.** Engage in past-life regressions to clear away leftover emotions that could be holding you back today. Read books and watch movies related to your past lives.

— **Be aware of the power of your temper.** When a Wise One slings anger toward another person, it's akin to casting a dark spell. Use your power carefully, and think twice before cursing someone, as this can hurt other people, as well as come back to haunt you.

— **Teach what's important to you.** You're always teaching by example. One reason to pull yourself up to your highest level is to inspire others. You elected to come to Earth to teach about human potential, so it's important for you to model that in your own life.

— **Laugh and play.** Even though you have a vital mission, it's important to inject regular doses of playfulness into your life. Sincerity, not seriousness, is called for in your mission. Laughter also helps you heal any heartbreak suffered in this life or past ones.

Chapter 8

If You Feel That You Fit into More Than One Category . . .

About 10 percent of my audience members who hear the description of the Earth Angel realms tell me, "I feel like I fit into more than one category!" These Earth Angels know that they're lightworkers, yet they're unclear about their particular realm. Here are some points to consider:

1. Energy: Tune in to your overall "energy blueprint"

The energy of a(n):	Is:
Incarnated Angel	Sweet and loving
Incarnated Elemental	Warm and playful
Starperson	Helpful and detached
Wise One	Serious, intense, and regal

2. Physical appearance

People in this realm:	Have these physical characteristics:
Incarnated Angels	Beautiful or cherubic faces with large bodies
Incarnated Elementals	Look like larger versions of fairies, elves, sprites, mermaids, leprechauns, etc.
Starpeople	Are tall and lanky; or short, with thin or large bodies. They have unusual eyes and facial features. Plain in dress, they wear minimal makeup.
Wise Ones	Long faces, with faraway expressions in their eyes. They wear dark-colored flowing shirts and dresses and often have long hair.

3. Interests

People in this realm:	Are focused on:
Incarnated Angels	Healing and service work; keeping relationships peaceful and happy.
Incarnated Elementals	Teaching, entertaining, the arts, and environmentalism.

| Starpeople | Energy healing, particularly Reiki; being helpful as needed. |
| Wise Ones | Teaching and practicing mystical, psychic, and Earth-based spirituality. |

A Note about Walk-Ins

You'll notice that the Walk-In realm is absent from the lists above. That's because a Walk-In's characteristics depend on the realm from which the person's body comes from, as well as the person's soul. Many Walk-Ins are "hybrids." For instance, you could have the body of an Incarnated Elemental (because the soul that walked-out was one) and the soul of a Starperson. Since your soul inherited the brain and body of another realm, you would feel influences from, and exhibit characteristics of, both realms.

That means you fit into three categories: the Walk-In realm, the realm your body originated from, and the realm of your soul. You'll want to pay attention to the information and guidance given for all three realms. It might mean that you feel extra-confused and disconnected periodically. However, keep your mission as your primary focus, and know that the rest is just details.

The Evolving Soul and the Dabbler

If you still don't know your realm, or your answers to the quiz in Chapter 2 were nonspecific, you may be an "Evolving Soul" or a "Dabbler." That means that you're either moving from one realm to the next, or are hopscotching through the realms for the sake of variety and growth.

— **The Evolving Soul:** If you're an Evolving Soul, you're moving from one realm to the next, so you may not identify with one particular group. Perhaps you've spent many lifetimes in one realm and have learned everything you can from this experience, so you elect to enter a new realm. You don't identify fully with the group you just left or the group you're newly joining.

If this sounds like you, give yourself time to adjust to the new group, and don't judge yourself harshly for feeling disconnected. Earth Angels in the Evolving Soul category can feel doubly alienated—not only do you feel separate from humans, but you feel different from the other Earth Angels as well! It can feel like being the last kid picked for a softball team: unwanted and unappreciated. Know that these are temporary feelings, and pray for spiritual assistance to know that you're not alone, and that you *are* wanted and appreciated. After all, you were very brave to switch to a new realm, and you probably did so out of the gallant intention to be extra-helpful to the world!

— **The Dabbler:** Some souls desire variety, excitement, and a wealth of experience. If you're a Dabbler, like "a kid in a candy store," you can't decide what you want, so you select everything on the menu. The Dabblers are Earth Angels who move from realm to realm. You never quite settle into one particular realm family. Instead, you graze from the highlights that each realm has to offer. Simultaneously, you bring gifts to each realm from the lessons you've learned while in the other Earth Angel realms. Dabblers rapidly adapt to new situations and people, much like children who move a lot and attend different schools, yet develop the ability to quickly fit in.

✦�֎✦

If you're an Evolving Soul or a Dabbler, you're like a honeybee going from flower to flower, taking and bringing nourishment as you travel. You provide valuable services because you infuse the realms with fresh blood, new ideas, and awakened vitality.

You could also be from a new realm that's yet undiscovered. As the world unfolds, new missions are required. And if you're one of the souls initiating those new missions, God bless you for your service!

Life-Path Work for Evolving Souls and Dabblers

Evolving Souls and Dabblers fall into two distinct groups: the Independent Thinkers and the Adaptors. Independent Thinkers are take-charge individuals and radical nonconformists who take pride in being outsiders. They believe that "normalcy" is tantamount to being sentenced to mediocrity. Independent Thinkers are champions of humanitarian and environmentalist causes—unless the causes are too popular. Independent Thinkers don't like to be trendy, and they desire their own unique niche outside of the mass populace.

Independent Thinkers, not surprisingly, do best in self-employment work geared around artistic or inventive pursuits. They don't enjoy systems, rules, or guidelines from outside "authorities." Ideal careers for Independent Thinkers would be the fine arts, craftwork, publishing, writing, or photography.

Dabblers love any career that offers them excitement and an opportunity to learn. They're better at working with the public than the Independent Thinkers. Ideal careers would be travel (working as a tour guide or working on a cruise ship), being a talent agent or scout (making other people's dreams come true), and any sales work involving a product or service that the Dabbler truly believes in.

Guidance and Suggestions If You're an Evolving Soul or a Dabbler

— **Respect your decision for independence.** Souls in this non-realm are generally nonconformists and rabble rousers. The earth needs your strength and power right now, so please don't dilute it by trying to fit in to any particular group (unless it comes naturally).

— **Teach freedom.** Too many humans allow themselves to be controlled by reigning authorities. By your refusal to conform or be tied down, you teach them alternatives. The more that you can do to garner personal happiness and peace, the more effective your teachings will be. Remember that you teach first by example, and then formal teaching opportunities arise as you allow them.

— **Manifest, manifest, manifest.** Because you tend to work outside of systems, you need to rely upon your personal manifestation power to sustain you materially. Remember that there are no neutral thoughts or words, so everything you say and think creates your future. Therefore, think about what you desire, and not about what you fear.

⇥✸⇤

Afterword

We're Counting on You!

Earth Angel, thank you for being on the planet at this time. With your great and loving energy, you're helping us just by being here! And yet—as you're well aware—you signed up for so much more. You elected to come here at a crucial time in the planet's history to effect great change, utilizing your natural resources of talents combined with harmonious actions.

Unless the mass populace takes a different approach to the environment and each other, life as we know it may not continue. You're here to teach alternatives. You'll know what to teach by noticing which issues fuel your passions, excitement, worry, or anger. For example, you might be here to teach how to manifest our material needs so that we don't compete, steal, or go to war to get our share. Or perhaps you're here to teach about the vital necessity of protecting our air, water, and soil quality. Maybe you contracted to teach healthier ways to raise and educate children. There are hundreds of vital topics to teach right now.

How do you teach? Any way that you can—for instance, by being a role model, by authoring books, writing articles, sending letters to editors of publications, taking action within educational and government systems, and/or by giving speeches or making media appearances.

One thing is clear: We need Earth Angels who are willing to be leaders. Old systems that lack integrity are beginning to fall, such as corporations and churches with histories of abuse. The new energy will no longer support or hide dark energy. Darkness within the educational, government, and legal systems will also cause them to wobble. As these changes occur, Earth Angel leaders (such as you) can guide people away from panic and pessimism, and toward a focus on letting the old be replaced with something better.

We're all counting on you to take the reigns of your life's purpose and embrace it fully. Any step that you take is helpful and sorely needed right now . . . provided that it comes from your intention to help. Please don't delay moving forward, waiting to figure out exactly what your mission is, what next step to take, or to receive an ironclad guarantee that you'll succeed. Doing *anything* that comes from love in your heart will be helpful, much like the ways small gifts given to a worthy cause eventually add up to a hefty donation. Start anywhere—just dive in!

Along the way, please take good care of your physical body. It's a very important tool in your mission. Yet, many Earth Angels such as yourself have never before had a physical body, so you may neglect or abuse it. By feeding it organic foods and beverages, exercising regularly, and getting adequate rest, you'll have more energy for your life's purpose.

A number of years ago, a very influential Earth Angel named Louise L. Hay (whom I've mentioned several times in this book—and who's the founder of Hay House, the publisher of this book) was guided to write about her insights into the link between physical ailments and underlying thoughts. Yet, not one publisher would print her materials! So instead of giving up, she typed and stapled several copies of the manuscript herself. Then, she felt urged to give workshops on the topic. At first, only two or three people came to her lectures. Today, that manuscript—*Heal Your Body*—has helped countless people, and was the basis for her *New York Times* bestselling book, *You Can Heal Your Life*, which has sold 16 million copies around the world. And now, when Louise gives a lecture, thousands of people attend!

Aren't you glad that Louise didn't get discouraged about her life's purpose? Aren't you grateful that she persevered? There are dozens of similar stories of people who have made the world a better place, and whose beginnings were quite humble.

✦❋✦

Your ego is a creation of fear, while your true self is a creation of love. Your ego's goals are aimed toward making you feel small, inadequate, and powerless. Yet how can a being who's made in the image and likeness of the Creator be *anything* but mighty, powerful, and wise?

Your ego knows that if you remember your true spiritual nature (perfect, powerful, creative, and intelligent), it will lose its power to frighten you, so it feeds you lies such as: "If you become powerful, you'll abuse that power. People won't like you as much. People will be jealous of you,"

and so on. Please, please don't listen to the ego!
Tell it to go sit in the corner and keep its rantings
to itself. Treat it like a buzzing fly, and don't focus
on it.

Remember that the bigger the purpose, the bigger the fear; there's a correlation. The more people
that you'll potentially help, the more force your ego
will use to hold you back. Your ego urges you to
delay your mission by preparing instead of doing.
Your ego says, "First you have to lose weight, make
more money, get married, get divorced, move,
graduate, get published, open a healing center, and
so forth . . . and *then* you'll be able to help the
world." What hogwash!

Earth Angel, you're ready right now for your
mission! There will never be a day more perfect
than today to work on it! Even though you may feel
unqualified or unprepared, do it anyway! Author
Sheldon Kopp once wrote, "I have never begun any
important venture for which I felt adequately prepared." In other words, you'll probably never feel
completely ready for your mission, so there's no
point in waiting.

Pray for daily assignments that tell you how
you can help make Earth a cleaner and more peaceful environment. Your prayers will be answered in

the form of opportunities for you to teach and heal. As these doors open for you, please don't turn and run the other way. You *are* ready. You *deserve* to do this beautiful work. And *you* are qualified . . . now!

Resources
for Earth Angels

Books for Incarnated Angels

There aren't any books that I'm aware of about Incarnated Angels (other than this book); however, here are some books that will be helpful for you if you're in this realm:

The Assertive Woman, by Stanlee Phelps and Nancy Austin (Impact Publishers, 1997)

When I Say No, I Feel Guilty, by Manuel J. Smith, Ph.D. (Bantam Books, 1975)

Your Perfect Right: Assertiveness and Equality in Your Life and Relationships, by Robert E. Alberti and Michael L. Emmons (Impact Publishers, 2001)

Support Groups for Incarnated Angels

Although the groups below aren't specifically for you Incarnated Angels, they can help you learn about assertiveness and boundaries, and give you support while you reclaim your personal power. Meetings are held throughout the world. You can get a list of these meetings by contacting:

Al-Anon
1600 Corporate Landing Parkway
Virginia Beach, VA 23454-5617
E-mail: WSO@al-anon.org
www.al-anon.org

Co-Dependents Anonymous
P.O. Box 33577
Phoenix, AZ 85067-3577
E-mail: info@codependents.org
www.codependents.org

Study Groups for *A Course in Miracles*

The book *A Course in Miracles* is a wonderful resource to help you heal from guilt. You may also find *Course* book-study groups a helpful support network. You can find a listing of study groups through:

Miracle Distribution Center
3947 E. La Palma Ave.
Anaheim, CA 92807
(714) 632-9005 • fax: (714) 632-9115
E-mail: info@miraclecenter.org
www.miraclecenter.org

Books for and about Incarnated Elementals

Summer with the Leprechauns: A True Story by Tanis Helliwell (Blue Dolphin Publishing, 1997)

Healing with the Fairies, by Doreen Virtue (Hay House, 2001)

Books about Walk-Ins

Strangers Among Us, by Ruth Montgomery
(Fawcett Publishing, 1984)

Walk-Ins/Soul Exchange, by Karyn K. Mitchell,
N.D., Ph.D. (Mind Rivers, 1999)

*Welcome to Planet Earth: A Guide for Walk-Ins
and Starseeds*, by Hannah Beaconsfield (Light
Technology Publishing, 1997)

A Support Group for Walk-Ins

WE International
Walk-Ins for Evolution
P. O. Box 28875
St. Paul, MN 55128
www.Walk-Ins.com

Books about Starpeople:

Aliens Among Us, by Ruth Montgomery
(Fawcett Publishing, 1986)

E.T. 101: The Cosmic Instruction Manual, by Zoev Jho and Diana Luppi (Intergalactic Council Publications, 1990)

Keepers of the Garden, by Dolores Cannon (Ozark Mountain Pub., 1993)

Star People, by Brad & Francie Steiger (Berkley Publishing Group, 1986)

Starborn, by Brad Steiger & Sherry Hansen Steiger (Berkley Publishing Group, 1992)

From Elsewhere: Being E.T. in America, by Scott Mandelker (Bantam Books, 1996)

Universal Vision: Soul Evolution and the Cosmic Plan, by Scott Mandelker (U.V. Way Publishing, 2000)

A Website Community for Starpeople

This Website provides a chat room, and information about being a "Wanderer," and is an excellent virtual support area for Starpeople: **www.alienation.com**

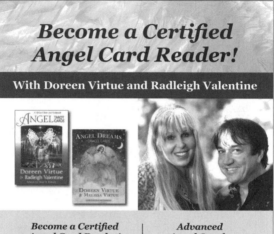

About the Author

Doreen Virtue is a doctor of psychology who now gives workshops on topics related to her books and oracle cards. She is the author of *The Care and Feeding of Indigo Children*, the *Healing with the Angels* book and oracle cards, and the *Messages from Your Angels* book and oracle cards, among many other works. She has appeared on *Oprah*, CNN, and *Good Morning America*; and has been featured in newspapers and magazines worldwide. For information on Doreen's workshops, please visit her Website at: **www.AngelTherapy.com**.

❖✳❖

Hay House Titles of Related Interest

BOOKS

Astrology Through a Psychic's Eyes, by Sylvia Browne

The Indigo Children: The New Kids Have Arrived,
by Lee Carroll and Jan Tober

*Sixth Sense: Including the Secrets of the Etheric
Subtle Body*, by Stuart Wilde

AUDIO PROGRAMS

*Angels and Spirit Guides: How to Call Upon Your Angels
and Spirit Guide for Help*, by Sylvia Browne

Angels! Angels! Angels!, by Denise Linn

Invocation of the Angels, by Joan Borysenko, Ph.D.

Understanding Your Angels and Meeting Your Guides,
by John Edward

All of the above are available at your local bookstore,
or may be ordered through Hay House, Inc.:

(800) 654-5126 or **(760) 431-7695**
(800) 650-5115 (fax) or **(760) 431-6948 (fax)**
www.hayhouse.com®

Notes

Notes

Notes

Notes

We hope you enjoyed this Hay House book. If you'd like to receive
our online catalog featuring additional information on Hay House
books and products, or if you'd like to find out more about
the Hay Foundation, please contact:

Hay House, Inc.
P.O. Box 5100
Carlsbad, CA 92018-5100

(760) 431-7695 or **(800) 654-5126**
(760) 431-6948 (fax) or **(800) 650-5115** (fax)
www.hayhouse.com® • **www.hayfoundation.org**

Published and distributed in Australia by: Hay House Australia Pty.
Ltd., 18/36 Ralph St., Alexandria NSW 2015 • *Phone:* 612-9669-4299
Fax: 612-9669-4144 • www.hayhouse.com.au

Published and distributed in the United Kingdom by: Hay House UK,
Ltd., Astley House, 33 Notting Hill Gate, London W11 3JQ
Phone: 44-20-3675-2450 • *Fax:* 44-20-3675-2451
www.hayhouse.co.uk

Published and distributed in the Republic of South Africa by: Hay
House SA (Pty), Ltd., P.O. Box 990, Witkoppen 2068 • *Phone/Fax:*
27-11-467-8904 • info@hayhouse.co.za • www.hayhouse.co.za

Published in India by: Hay House Publishers India, Muskaan
Complex, Plot No. 3, B-2, Vasant Kunj, New Delhi 110 070 • *Phone:*
91-11-4176-1620 • *Fax:* 91-11-4176-1630 • www.hayhouse.co.in

Distributed in Canada by: Raincoast Books, 2440 Viking Way,
Richmond, B.C. V6V 1N2 • *Phone:* 1-800-663-5714
Fax: 1-800-565-3770 • www.raincoast.com